Women and Community in Oman

Women
and
Community in Oman

CHRISTINE EICKELMAN

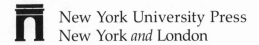 New York University Press
New York *and* London

Library of Congress Cataloging in Publication Data

Eickelman, Christine, 1944–
    Women and community in Oman.

    Bibliography: p.
    Includes index.
    1. Women—Oman—Social conditions.   2. Oman—Social
life and customs.   I. Title.
HQ1731.E35   1984   305.4'2'905353   84-974
ISBN 0-8147-2165-6 (alk. paper)
ISBN 0-8147-2166-4 (pbk.)

c 10 9 8 7 6 5 4 3 2
p 10 9 8 7 6 5 4 3 2

Clothbound editions of New York University Press books are Smyth-sewn
and printed on permanent and durable acid-free paper.

To Amal and Dale

CONTENTS

LIST OF TABLES AND ILLUSTRATIONS

PREFACE

I arrived in Oman in early September 1979 with my husband and nineteenth-month old daughter. My husband, an anthropologist, had received a National Science Foundation grant to do research in inner Oman on ideas of leadership and political authority.

After a brief stay in the capital area, we moved to Hamra, an oasis located on the western edge of the Jabal al-Akhdar region of inner Oman, with a population of about 2,500 in 1980. Hamra is the tribal capital of the 'Abriyin where the leader of the tribe and many other notables reside. I remained in Hamra through March 1980 and returned subsequently in September-October 1980.

As in many parts of the Muslim world, men and women in inner Oman are separated for large parts of the day. I knew before we left for Oman that my husband could not interview women nor participate in any of their social activities. I came to the oasis, therefore, with the intention of leaning about the daily life, concerns and aspirations of women in the Omani interior and the roles they play in the community. I was also interested in how they interpret and accommodate to the rapid changes taking place in Arabian society today.

This was my first trip to the Arab Gulf but not to the Middle East. In 1968–70 I had lived with my husband in Egypt and in Iraq and I had engaged with him in fieldwork in Morocco. I had a background in anthropology and Middle East studies and could read modern literary Arabic. During my two years in the Arab world I had learned colloquial Moroccan Arabic and some Egyptian Arabic. I was thus able to understand Omani Arabic very quickly after my arrival.

Fieldwork experience in Morocco had taught me the extreme importance of keeping fieldnotes, the daily recording of one's conversations, actions, observations and impressions. The greater part of this book is based on daily notes I kept while in Oman. In many chapters I include quotations from these notes in order to retain a sense of detail, dialogue and immediacy that is often lost in anthropological analysis. I date these fieldnote quotations to show the importance of time in reconstructing the past and my record of understanding. These quotations also attest to the immense importance of detail—small phrases perhaps made in passing, facial expressions, persons and social relations at first not well known—whose significance grows clear over time.

After living for several months in the oasis, I began to discern the meaning and context of such basic concepts as family, privacy, work, propriety, status and sociability. These were the notions by which people made sense of their lives and understood the actions of others. Although I came to understand these concepts mostly through my shared daily life with Omani women, I explain how they are held in large part by Omani men as well.

In recent years the relation of anthropologists with the people with whom they live and work and the mutual perceptions of anthropologists and those whose lives they seek to interpret have been topics of concern. For this reason, the first chapter describes my initial reaction to Oman, how I became aware of Hamra's main social divisions, the principal events that led to the growth of close ties with certain households and how women of the oasis perceived me and my daughter. Later chapters introduce the social world of women. I begin with the small, intimate circle of the household, then the wider family network, neighbors, and finally, formal visiting in the community at large and the significance of women's visiting networks for maintaining oasis unity. Chapter 7 discusses children, motherhood and childrearing because these are such important aspects of women's lives and of their identity.

Once, when I was discussing marriages with a woman in Hamra, someone interrupted us to ask, "Why does she want to know this?" The woman with whom I had been conversing answered briefly, "She is trying to understand." I wrote this book with a sense of obligation to the women of Hamra, empathy for them as persons, and respect for their trust in me. I am therefore interpreting their society as much as possible from what I perceive to be their perspective and not one abstractly derived from the concerns of my own society.

Despite its contemporary strategic significance, Oman remains less well known to Westerners than neighboring states, such as Saudi Arabia. Hence a brief description situates my own experience with the country in a wider context. Located in the southeastern part of the Arabian peninsula, Oman is surrounded to the north by the United Arab Emirates, to the west by Saudi Arabia and to the southwest by the Peoples' Democratic Republic of Yemen.

Geographically, ethnically, and religiously Oman is one of the more complex states of the Arabian peninsula. Its major regions include the southern province of Dhofar; the Batina coast, the fertile coastal plain of northern Oman; and inner Oman, a string of oasis towns and villages located in the valleys and foothills of the Hajar mountain range. The coastal ports and oases along the Batina coast have a multiethnic, polyglot population that has lived for generations by seafaring, trade and fishing. The towns and oases of the interior have almost exclusively tribal populations. Until the advent of economic opportunities created by oil wealth in Oman and neighboring countries, most of the tribes of the interior lived from agriculture and some livestock herding. This subsistence livelihood was supplemented in this century by migrant labor to East Africa and to Bahrain.

Ibadism has been a major factor in distinguishing

Oman from its neighbors. Most of the population of the Omani interior is Ibadi Muslim, together with a significant part of the coastal population. The third major orientation in Islam together with the Sunni and Shi'a, Ibadism originated in the eighth century C.E., in the course of disputes over succession to the leadership of the Islamic community. Most Ibadi beliefs are similar to those of Sunni Muslims, but the Ibadi have in the past firmly rejected the notion of dynastic rule, even that of descendants of the Prophet Muhammad. Instead, they selected the person most qualified by reason of piety and religious training as their spiritual and temporal leader (*imām*) without regard to descent. Although the imamate ceased effectively to exist in the 1700s, when the present dynasty, the Al Bu Sa'id, came into power, it was revived in the interior in the twentieth century. The last three imams ruled in Nizwa from 1913 to 1955, when the interior was assimilated into the administration of the late Sultan Sa'id bin Taymur (r. 1932–1970).

The second half of Sultan Sa'id bin Taymur's reign was a period of extreme isolation for Oman, an isolation that was all the more striking when contrasted with the transformations that surrounding Gulf nations were undergoing with their new oil economy. The country was closed to all foreigners save for a handful of British military officials and oil company personnel. Even after Oman began to receive oil revenues in 1967, the former Sultan refused to use these funds for the development of his country. After 1957 a growing number of Omani men emigrated to neighboring countries, seeking work, education and, for some, political refuge. It was only in 1970, with the coming to power of the present Sultan Qabus bin Sa'id, that Oman opened its doors to development. Sultan Qabus has built a large infrastructure of roads, schools, hospitals, communications, defense and government offices essential for a modern nation.

The meaning of change is an important theme present throughout my book. Economic and political changes of the last decades are effectively transforming oases of the interior of Oman into satellites of the coastal capital area. In my last chapter I shift perspective from looking at Omani notions of community and society to a more general discussion of the historical, economic and political transformations that Hamra has undergone in the last decades, and how these changes are clearly visible in the shifting spatial layout of the oasis. At the risk of disconcerting academic readers I have chosen not to discuss these issues first because the present order more accurately represents how I came to understand Omani society today. In fact, in retrospect, I strongly feel that one can understand these changes only by trying to approximate first how Omanis think of their own society and seek to explain their actions to themselves and to others.

At the same time, the oil economy has not led so far to dramatic transformations in how people deal with one another. The concepts that I analyze in this book continue to be the basis of daily, interpersonal relations. The fact that these concepts are flexible enough to accommodate and make sense of major economic and political shifts is one reason for the striking self-confidence of people living in the interior of Oman. Few persons appear disoriented at the rapid self-transformations of their society in the wake of oil revenues.

In transliterating Arabic words, I have used the system of the *International Journal of Middle East Studies*, without diacritics, except for words commonly used in English. Arabic words and terms however, are fully transliterated in the glossary and upon their first occurrence in the text. Rather than burden the reader with Arabic plurals, I generally add an *s* to the singular form.

Many people have helped me in the course of living in Oman and in writing this book. I am grateful for their encouragement, suggestions and comments. Elizabeth Warnock Fernea of the University of Texas at Austin and Hildred Geertz of Princeton University read an earlier version of this book and provided insightful comments.

Farhad Kazemi of New York University was the first to invite me to talk on my work at the Hagop Kevorkian Center for Middle Eastern Studies of New York University. From this lecture and others that followed I received many suggestions and ideas. Annette B. Weiner and Bayly Winder both of New York University showed continued support for my work and provided useful comments.

William Beeman, Constance Cronin, Bonnie Glover, William Royce, Marjorie Rütimann, Constance Sutton and Delores Walters have read versions of this book or parts of it and gave me helpful advice. I am grateful to Michael Bonine of the University of Arizona who prepared the maps and to Birgitte Grue of *Aktuelt* (Copenhagen), for use of photographs she took of Hamra while visiting Oman under the auspices of the Ministry of Information.

It is not possible to thank individually all the people in Oman who have been helpful to me. Let me thank in particular His Excellency Khalfan Nasser al-Wahaiby, Minister of Social Affairs and Labour at the time of my stay in Oman. Most of my contact with him was through my husband, but he showed a sustained interest in our work and gave us intellectual and practical support when we needed it most. I am also grateful to Muhsin Juma of the Ministry of Social Affairs and Labour and his wife. They generously gave us hospitality in their home each time we visited the capital area and they followed our work with interest. I would like to thank Shaykh 'Abdalla Muhanna al-'Abri and all the people of Hamra for their continued hospitality, generosity, tolerance and patience. Since the polite Omani asks few direct questions and the anthropologist asks many, I must have seemed very rude or at least indiscreet many times. To protect the privacy of persons with whom I worked, all names are fictitious save that of Shaykh 'Abdalla who is a public figure by virtue of his tribal responsibilities.

This book would not have been possible without the continued support of my husband, Dale Eickelman. He shared fieldwork with me, gave me detailed comments on several versions of the manuscript, and allowed me the use of his notes and other materials. In a reversal of standard acknowledgements between husband and wife, in this instance, I can thank *him* for entering the final version of this book into his word processor.

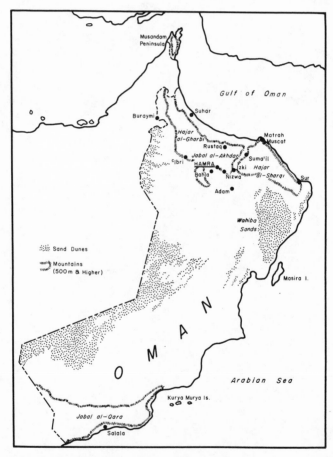

Figure 1. Map of Oman. Adapted from a map in the JOURNAL OF OMAN STUDIES, vol. 5, 1979.

1.

BEGINNINGS

A GLARING, blinding sun. Damp, clammy heat. Dust often as thick as fog. Except for a narrow strip of carefully tended shrubs and flowers in the median strip of the highway leading from the airport to the capital, the entire region seemed devoid of vegetation. Odd-shaped rocky hills and plains lined the entire thirty-seven kilometers of road linking Sib Airport with the port of Matrah, the capital area's older center of trade and commerce, and Muscat, the old, walled administrative center. Elegant villas, shops, and tall apartment buildings in various stages of completion rose from this barren, moonlike environment. The appearance of Matrah's waterfront, a row of white buildings, modern and old, set off by a newly constructed corniche and the blue sea, was comforting because it was more familiar. The smell of fish mingled with that of car fumes. In the distance, I could just make out oil tankers riding at anchor. It was one o'clock on a day in early September, and few people were in the streets. Our guest house in Matrah, nine years old but the oldest in Oman, catered mostly to Arab, Indian, and Pakistani businessmen. It was run more like a rooming house than a hotel, and the staff, mostly Indian, were delighted with the presence of our nineteen-month-old daughter. Guests who brought children along were rare, and the families of the staff were back in India.

Three days later we moved temporarily to Ruwi, a new town created in the early 1970s in the valley, inland from Matrah. There we settled into a comfortable apartment generously loaned to us by an Omani who was on vacation. We remained there until we were able to make the necessary arrangements for our move into the interior, where we were to conduct anthropological fieldwork.

I found Ruwi very different from other Middle Eastern cities that I knew. Barely ten years old, this extension of Matrah depends completely on motor transport. The dust, the uneven ground, the lack of sidewalks, large distances between buildings, and the heat made walking arduous and virtually impossible for women like me with small children. Save for some Indian servants and workmen, few people were on foot. Looking out of my apartment windows, I could see barren hills, a highway, and the side of another apartment building that was a replica of ours. The city was silent. Where were the street vendors, the children, the small shops, the crowds of men, the blaring radios, the prayer calls, and the women on their balconies or roof terraces so characteristic of neighborhoods in other Middle Eastern and North African cities? While my husband met various officials and arranged for housing in the interior and the purchase of a car, I remained alone with my daughter for long stretches of the day. We were lonely.

There was a modest but adequate bus service between Ruwi and Matrah, used mostly by Indians. I went a few times to the Matrah market, carrying Amal, my daughter, and a thermos of water. No one paid much attention to me in my cotton blouse and maxi skirt, with a kerchief covering my hair. Merchants were courteous. Buying was straightforward with no bargaining, unlike elsewhere in the Middle East. The sidewalks were busy without being overly crowded. Many men wore elegant, dazzlingly white, long tunics (*dishdāsha*s), their heads covered with skullcaps or turbans. Others wrapped a checkered Madras skirt (*wizār*) around their waists, with a T-shirt above. Save for some young Indians wearing European trousers and close-fitting shirts, no men wore Western-type clothes. A few women were in the downtown market area as well, some wrapped from head to foot in long black cloaks (*'abāya*s), but not all women wore one. I have the vivid image in my mind of a woman on Matrah's main street carrying a young child in her arms and walking a few feet behind a man. She wore a shawl and a boldly patterned tunic over embroidered pantaloons. The brightness of the synthetic fabrics made me observe her a few seconds. Suddenly she turned toward me and gave me a wide, friendly grin. I could not yet tell from her clothes to what ethnic or religious group she belonged, but I knew that Oman's coastal population was extremely diversified. There were Arabs, Baluchis, Liwatiya, Persians, Indians, and people of African origin. The population was also divided along religious lines: Sunni Muslims, Ibadi Muslims, Persian Shi'i Muslims, Indian Shi'i Muslims, and some Hindus. There were also many foreigners: Egyptians, Jordanians, Saudis, East Africans, a sea of Indians, Pakistanis, and Bangladeshis, and—rarely on the streets—a scattering of Europeans and Americans.

Late afternoon and early evening are visiting hours in the area around Muscat. We were invited and received extremely well by many people during our first few days in Oman. I asked many of the women I encountered for information about what food and supplies I would find in the interior, but no one seemed to have spent more than a few hours away from the coastal area. Many of the men were equally uninformed. Some persons spoke of the harsh material conditions we would find, the poor distribution of food, the heat, the difficulties of living without electricity. I began to worry.

Soon I met my close neighbors in the apartment building. Amal played regularly in the lobby, which was cool and well ventilated, and other children came to join her. I was immediately drawn to my young and smiling neighbor Rayya, and I think she reciprocated my feelings. Her clothes were a sea of large, bold designs, in the brightest colors, which to me seemed to have been chosen to compensate for the bleakness and lack of color in the natural landscape. Rayya was shy at first, but soon she became vivacious and talkative when she realized that I understood Arabic. She came from Sur, a coastal city to the south, had four children, and had lived for five years with her husband in Abu Dhabi. She invited me in for tea, recognized how lonely I was, and soon introduced me to her morning activities. No other "Europeans" lived in the building or the immediate neighborhood. She showed me her clothes and snapshots of her relatives in Sur, and taught me how to cook rice and fish Omani style. We discussed children at length, and I helped her prepare school clothes for her eldest daughter, who was entering first grade that fall.

Rayya introduced me to my first coffee-drinking session with some of the women of the apartment building. One of these women was the wife of Shaykh Sa'id of Hamra, the oasis where we were planning to do our fieldwork.[1]

> September 19. Shaykh Sa'id's wife and daughter again visited one of the neighbors on our floor, a family from Qal'a. They came around noon, when most of the cooking was done, but before their husbands were expected at the end of the government workday of two P.M. Shaykh Sa'id's wife was wrapped loosely in a black 'abaya and carried a large tray of fresh dates on her head. Her daughter, around sixteen, wore a light blue veil, a tunic, and machine-embroidered pantaloons, and carried a large thermos of coffee. The lady from Qal'a invited Rayya for coffee.

Since I was present, I was also invited. We ig-
nored the Western-style couch and armchairs,
standard government issue, and sat instead on a
large carpet. There were no introductions. We
were served mouth-watering fresh yellow dates
and sliced bananas. Coffee was poured into a
small Chinese cup, and each of us took a turn
drinking. As long as I did not refuse the cup, it
was refilled and returned to me. Part of the
conversation was about a film on television the
night before, although I had difficulty in understanding some of the things said. Shaykh Sa'id's
daughter commented on my clothes and how
plain they were. There was also talk of eye infec-
tions. Rayya brought out her daughter's new
school uniform, which everyone admired.
Shaykh Sa'id's wife did not speak to me directly
but seemed to find my presence amusing. Every
time I spoke she looked at me with a twinkle
and seemed to suppress a peal of laughter.

Later I asked Rayya whether she knew many women
in the building. "No," she answered, "just these
women." Yet her balcony had a view of the entrance
lobby to our building, and she could name me many
others. She did not think highly of the family from
Qal'a, although she visited them when Shaykh Sa'id's
wife came. She privately complained to me about the
children, their dirt and their lack of manners (adab).

She told me Shaykh Sa'id's wife was named
Miryam and that whenever she visited, she brought

large trays of dates and other fruits that she left behind. I had seen a similar plate of dates in Rayya's
refrigerator and wondered how many people Miryam
visited in this flamboyant manner. Was this distribution of fruit one of the duties of being a shaykh's wife?
How did one become part of a visiting network?

In addition to Rayya's family and the other from
Qal'a living on our floor, there was a bachelor (our
absent host) and a Jordanian family in a fourth apartment. The Jordanians received us very hospitably.
Dale knew the husband through his ministry friends,
and Amal played with their children. The wife, a
schoolteacher who was not home for extensive portions of the day, never took part in these coffee-drinking sessions.

The apartment building next to ours housed police officers and their families. A small playground
next to our house was reserved for their use. I used it,
unaware at first that it was restricted. Amal and I
found it difficult not to go out for long stretches of the
day. In the late afternoons it was the only area where
we could be outside with other children. Within a
week we became accepted at the playground and I met
other women from the interior.

September 19. On arriving at the playground,
women shake hands with those already sitting
down, exchanging polite, barely audible greetings. They are quite formal, and conversation is
general and not very intense. Many women sit
alone silently, some embroidering head caps

(*qimma*s) for men. Today I went around the playground and shook hands with everyone, just as
the others were doing. I spoke with two young
sisters who came from Nizwa, the largest oasis
of the interior and close to where we wanted to
live. One lives in Matrah, the other in Ruwi, and
they visit each other regularly. We introduced
ourselves and talked mostly about our children.
They seem to return regularly to Nizwa.

September 24. Now I automatically receive the
ritual handshakes from new arrivals. Small talk
with some women more talkative or curious
than others is more frequent than it was a few
days ago. Do I have only one child? Am I pregnant? Where do I come from? What does my
husband do? Do I work? Today I was taken for
an Egyptian, which surprised me, given my
thick accent in Arabic with a French overlay.
When I said I came from America, I heard someone say that Americans were "good"
(*kwayyis*), using the Egyptian word.

September 27. As soon as I arrived in the playground, a tall, handsome woman of about my
age came up and invited me to her house. A
Baluchiya from Matrah with six children, she
has been living in the police complex for the last
five years. She told me that other women in the
building came from all over Oman. They all
know one another and visit often. She knew my

neighbor Rayya by name, as well as Rayya's eldest son. After coffee, we returned together to
the playground, where we shook hands all
around. Some women no longer stare, and one
woman even asked me where I had been for the
last two days. "We have been visiting," I answered, smiling.

Rayya and I saw each other frequently during the
three weeks preceding our departure to the interior.
We drank coffee three times with Miryam, twice in the
apartment of Fadila, the woman from Qal'a. The last
time, the visit took place on a lower floor in the apartment of a woman from Rustaq, a large oasis about one
hour away from Muscat. This family was obviously of
a higher status because the coffee-drinking session
was more elaborate and formal. This was to be my last
contact with women of the interior living in the capital
before our move to Hamra.

October 2. Around 11:30 A.M., Fadila invited
Rayya and me to drink coffee downstairs with
Miryam. Our host, a woman from Rustaq, had
an older woman at her side who looked like her
mother. This time the fruits were provided by
the people from Rustaq—large trays of bananas,
watermelons, dates, and coffee. Miryam was offered the first cup of coffee. Fadila was offered
the second cup but refused, insisting that the
older woman from Rustaq be served first. Then
Fadila was served, followed by me and Rayya.

The television was on, and some children were crying, which made it difficult for me to follow the details of the conversation. Miryam was talking about me in a corner. They also discussed clothes for the coming feast and offered tips on how to take care of children's hair. "You will eat a lot of meat during the feast in Hamra," Miryam ventured, addressing me directly for the first time. Incense was burned in a small charcoal brazier, and a tray of perfume was placed before us. Everyone applied a little perfume on themselves from each bottle. As I was leaving the apartment, I noticed two young girls in their teens who had stayed quietly in the bedroom and had not taken part in the coffee-drinking session. They smiled at me and Amal.

We left for the interior on a Friday morning. Our small car was packed tightly with suitcases, a typewriter, tinned and dried foods, pots, pans, and other household goods, and a month's supply of disposable diapers. The road stretched before us in a straight line through a rocky plain with sparse vegetation, flanked by hills of bare rocks. The road began to curve more as we entered the Suma'il Gap, the traditional route that cuts through the Hajar mountain range and provides access to Nizwa. I still had little idea of what was behind those hills.

As we passed small oases with their mud-brick houses and tiny patches of gardens and date palms, I tried to imagine what Hamra would be like. Traffic was not heavy, but occasional roadside shacks selling soft drinks and gasoline stations indicated that the road was regularly used. I had an odd mixture of feelings: relief to be leaving the humid heat and barren landscape of the capital area, sadness for leaving some people behind, and anxiety and curiosity over what would happen next.

Two-and-a-half hours later we arrived at Nizwa, the largest oasis of the interior and until 1955 the capital of the Ibadi imamate. Nizwa is a vast oasis, with gardens of date trees and at its center, next to the crowded market, a large, stone fortress. Nothing I had seen earlier on the road prepared me for its size. The road skirted the market area, packed with people, animals, and flimsy fruit and vegetable stands in front of the most established shops. Its parking lot was filled with cars and trucks, and traffic slowed to a crawl.

Just over twenty kilometers past Nizwa, we turned sharply to the right. A green sign marked "al-Hamra" pointed to a feeder road, which, like the main one, was obviously new. The paved road leading to Hamra was not yet built when Dale first visited it the year before. By now, in addition to the barren hills on either side of the road, we could see the Jabal al-Akhdar, or "Green" Mountains, in front of us. We drove for about twenty minutes. Then the paved road was replaced abruptly by a gravel one. We climbed the rough gravel road up a hill. Just over its crest I got my first view of the oasis of Hamra, nestled at the foot of an enormous, grayish-green rock devoid of vegeta-

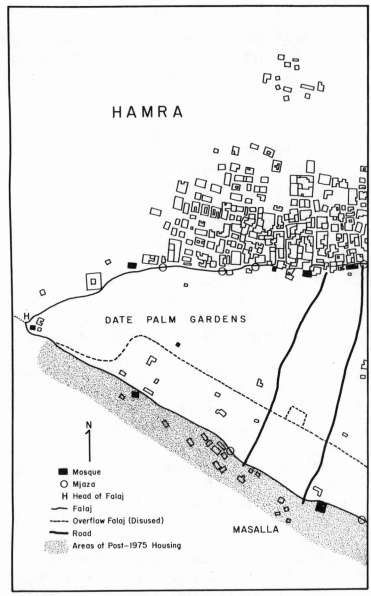

HAMRA

DATE PALM GARDENS

H

N

MASALLA

■ Mosque
O Mjaza
H Head of Falaj
— Falaj
--- Overflow Falaj (Disused)
▬ Road
░ Areas of Post–1975 Housing

Figure 2. Map of Hamra. Based on sketch by Dale F. Eickelman from

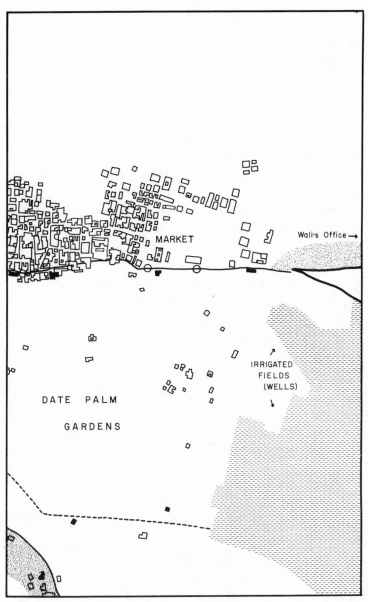

MARKET

Wali's Office →

IRRIGATED
FIELDS
(WELLS)

DATE PALM

GARDENS

a 1976 aerial photograph. Base: V5 SOAF986 50mm. × 2.

tion. Compared with its immediate surroundings, Hamra appeared lush and fertile, a small green jewel.

We drove on, passing a small hill with a dilapidated stone watchtower, a relic of a not-too-distant period when tribal warfare was endemic. Finally, we reached the date-palm gardens. Only the orchards separated us from the main part of town. We had to circle the gardens on a narrow, dusty road, which followed the *falaj,* or irrigation canal, on the edge of the gardens. On the other side of the road there were small houses. Many seemed to have been built fairly recently because they were made of cement, but all were modest in appearance.

We arrived in Hamra at noon. Few people were outside. A man wearing a Madras cotton wizar and a woman in a large, fringed colorful shawl, long tunic, and pantaloons looked at our car curiously. We stopped next to a small white mosque shaded by an enormous tree. A few children were bathing in the falaj next to it. The water seemed cool and inviting. We entered the gardens on a narrow path with a branch of the falaj and high mud-brick walls on either side. Fifteen yards in we came to a new metal door, brightly painted in green and yellow. It contrasted sharply with the crumbling mud wall in which it was embedded. This was the entrance to our new home: three separate buildings with a small cement courtyard. One building was a narrow, long room for receiving guests, the *sabla;* it had a small private room at one end. Another building was a kitchen and bathroom. The third contained a large room, which we used for sleeping. The other rooms of this building, to which we did not have access, were reserved for the use of the landlord's family. They had earlier been used by his grandsons, who were now studying in the capital area.

The contrast between our new home and our Ruwi apartment of the previous three weeks was staggering. Here we were surrounded on all sides by vegetation. Lime trees, banana trees, and date palms shaded the courtyard and buildings and made them wonderfully cool. Because repairs to our compound were not yet completed, the courtyard was in great disorder. Tools were strewn about, and there was a pile of sand in one corner. An enormous kerosene refrigerator that turned out to be broken lay on its side in another corner. Limes had fallen from the trees and had not yet been picked up.

Soon after we arrived, we were greeted formally by Shaykh 'Abdalla Muhanna al-'Abri, the tribal leader of the 'Abriyin, who was also our landlord. Shaykh 'Abdalla was in his sixties, with a white beard, and dressed in a spotless white dishdasha girded at the waist with a leather belt, a silver dagger, and a submachine gun. Coffee and dates were served, and we were then led back to his car, on the road near our house, for lunch at his house.

Shaykh 'Abdalla, like many other notables of the 'Abriyin, lived in a large, fortresslike mud-brick house that directly faced the orchards and was next to the falaj. A television aerial was visible from his roof terrace. We were led into a very dark first floor and into a

long, narrow guest room where several men were sitting. It looked like the beginning of a formal meal; so I
immediately asked the shaykh to introduce me and
my restless two-year-old to his family. This turned out
to be the right thing to do. As I began to follow a
young man up an extremely narrow, dark, and uneven stone stairway, carrying Amal in my arms, someone whispered, "She knows."

I entered a large, poorly lit room that had a dirt
floor. At one end low windows with metal bars gave
some light, and carpets had been spread next to the
windows. The room looked like a large vestibule.
Doors on either side led into side rooms. In the center
stood a tank of water with a small tap for washing.
Save for the carpets, probably of Indian origin, and a
ceiling fan that was not turned on but that indicated
the presence of an electric generator, the room was
devoid of furnishings and wall decorations. Nothing
seemed to point to the high status of our host.

Amal and I were expected. About ten women of
all ages immediately surrounded us. What I noticed
first was that many of them had their foreheads and
upper cheekbones daubed with a dark red substance,
which I first took to be henna. It turned out to be
mahaleb (*maḥlab*), an herb that is the same color as
henna when diluted with water, but which washes off
easily. One slender young woman had drawn a thin
red line across her forehead. It contrasted sharply
with her pale skin and kohl-blackened eyes. Some
women wore gold nose rings in one nostril. Others
wore earrings. Everyone's hair was black, oiled, parted

in the middle, and covered by a light, gauzelike synthetic veil (*wiqāya*, literally protection). The pantaloons were extremely tight at the ankles, requiring a zipper to allow the foot to fit through.

From the beginning it was clear that we were all curious and that I looked as extraordinary to these women as they did to me.

October 5. I met two older women who introduced themselves as Shaykh 'Abdalla's wives. They were with a large group of younger women. Some of them were the shaykh's daughters. Others were his son's wives, and still others his granddaughters or grandsons' wives. Each woman greeted me by a handshake and introduced herself quickly as "Ahmad's wife" or "Muhammad's daughter," rather than by her personal name. A large number of children of all ages were running about, lending an air of festivity and informality to this first meeting. One of the shaykh's wives pointed to groups of children, saying, "These are Ahmad's sons," or, "These are Muhammad's children." In response to my question, she pointed out her own children and those of other women and told me their personal names. The women were talkative and patient, repeating the information as much as I wanted.

Two young women sat whispering side by side. They appeared eager to talk to me. The one with the red band of mahaleb across her forehead was Sharifa, daughter of Shaykh 'Abdalla. Shaykha, sitting next to her, was a daughter of Shaykh Ibrahim, one of Shaykh 'Abdalla's brothers. She was married to one of Shaykh 'Abdalla's grandsons and Sharifa to a son of Shaykh Ibrahim. In spite of her youth, Sharifa said she had given birth four times. Shaykha had no children and was a student in the local intermediate school. She had a Peace Corps volunteer as an English teacher and spoke a few words of English. We talked about kinship, but there seemed to be such multiple ways people were related that I decided to resume discussions of this topic some other time.

Some of the conversation centered on Amal and me. To my surprise, Amal's curly black hair immediately drew comments. "She is different from you," someone said. I explained, as best as I could, that she was adopted. Questions flew. Did I have to pay for her? Did I know her mother? The first question puzzled me, but I answered "no" to both questions. Some women gave Amal great looks of pity when I said that I did not know her mother. Other women showed surprise that I did not wear makeup, that my hair was short and not parted exactly in the middle, and that neither Amal nor I wore jewelry.

Coffee and fruits were served in trays on the rug of this large room. Amal quickly helped herself to some fruits. There were many flies

buzzing around the fruits, and I silently hoped
that she would remain healthy. For lunch, we
were ushered into a side room where a plate of
rice cooked in meat broth with a huge piece of
goat meat on top was waiting for us. A side dish
of stewed onions was spread over the rice. One
of the shaykh's wives, perhaps the oldest, although they both looked close in age, ate with
us and cut up pieces of meat with her fingers. I
slowly began to eat. I was unsure of etiquette
and wanted to see whether she ate certain foods
first, perhaps the rice and onions, as was the
case in Morocco, where meat is eaten after the
vegetables. The woman looked up at me, surprised at the slowness of my eating, and asked
whether the food was good. "Yes," I smiled, and
proceeded to eat more quickly since I could discern no pattern in eating. Amal licked happily
on a goat bone. We spoke very little, and I was
then ushered back into the large room, where I
rinsed my hands, and returned to the carpeted
area.

It was at that first meeting that I became Miryam
to the women of Hamra. My daughter's name, Amal,
was easily remembered by all the women because it
was Arabic. Everyone kept forgetting my name and
made me repeat it. Women in Morocco had the same
difficulty with my name. They spontaneously approx-
imated it with Kristal, the brand name of a local cooking oil. My second name is Marie (Miryam in Arabic),

and I mentioned this to one of the women in the room. She immediately said, "Miryam is a good name." From then on I was called Miryam in Hamra.

My first afternoon in Hamra I went to collect drinking water from the head of the falaj, our only source of potable water. It was barely a three-minute walk from our house, but we went by car. There was no way I could carry, even for that short distance, our large plastic containers filled with water. Yet this was a woman's chore. My husband discreetly stopped our car a short distance away in order not to infringe on an area where only women could move freely. Many women were walking back and forth with buckets of water gracefully balanced on their heads. Others stood in line waiting their turn. I recognized several faces from the shaykhly household I had visited earlier in the day. No one showed surprise at my presence, for news of our arrival had spread all over town. I took my place in line. Everyone greeted me with a smile and a firm handshake.

There was a great deal of laughter and talking among women as they waited their turn. One woman courteously took my two plastic containers and showed me where to stand in the stream in order to catch the fastest and cleanest running water. The water that flowed out from underground was clear and amazingly warm. I could make out little fishes swimming in the shadows of the underground canal. Another woman pointed out where the washing was done, a few feet away.

The self-confidence of the women was obvious. Going to the falaj was part of the oasis life. It was clear that it I was to live here, I was expected to draw my own water as soon as I learned how to do it properly and to handwash my own clothes. Henceforth I did just that; however, I continued to carry the water home by car. Once home, I poured part of this water into porous clay jars that hung on pegs in our courtyard. These jars were made in Bahla, a neighboring oasis known for their manufacture, and they cooled water very effectively.

The following day my immediate neighbors invited me to their house. A slim young woman ushered Amal and me into a courtyard shaded by an enormous mango tree and then into a large, rectangular room, one side of which had low windows cut from the thick, cool mud wall. They provided a wonderful view of the orchards.

> October 6. My neighbor's household consisted of a young woman, Nasra, her husband, a daughter of eighteen months, an infant son about six weeks old, and her husband's mother, Badriyya, a tall and large-boned woman in her early sixties. There may have been other people living in the house also, because other children and some older women were present whom I found it difficult to identify. A woman in her early thirties, Rashida, was also there. She had no living children (one had died) and lived in the house next to mine on the other side. We had coffee and dates. I was also served home-made yogurt spiced with a few grains of hot red peppers and some waferlike bread (*nkhāl*) that

Nasra made. The children seemed afraid of me. They clung to their mothers and older sisters and hid under their head shawls.

Infant mortality appears to have been very high in the past. One older woman told me with a sad face that she had ten children, but that only three were still alive. I also discovered that when I asked women the number of children they had, they usually included their dead children.

On the third day of our stay, Shaykh 'Abdalla invited us to lunch a second time. He was entertaining tribesmen from Misfa, a neighboring village in the mountains.

October 7. The women from Misfa were heavily jeweled with gold and silver and wore wristwatches, and their foreheads were decorated with red mahaleb and yellow saffron. Once again I ate in a side room with the tribal women and Nura, one of the shaykh's daughters. The meal consisted of chickens boiled with onions and tomato paste over rice. Each person added hot peppers and lime juice to her own portion of the communal plate.

When we finished eating, we returned to the central guest room and in sequence were served coffee, dates, chickpeas, sweets, and bananas. Eating patterns seemed quite complicated. Several rice trays were prepared, and different groups of people apparently ate separately. The village women paid little attention to me. Whatever the reason for their visit, it was not discussed in my presence. One of the village women once glanced at Amal. One of the shaykh's wives immediately explained to her that she was not my "natural" daughter (*ma bintha*). "I didn't give birth to her, but she is my daughter," I corrected. Without paying any attention to my remark, the village woman replied to the older shaykhly woman, "She is the daughter of a descendant of a slave (fem., *khādima*; pl., *khuddām*)." [At the time I took the term khadima to mean "servant," the meaning in classical Arabic, rather than the local meaning of "slave."] "Oh, no, she is not," I interrupted a second time. The two women looked at me rather dubiously, but since I spoke categorically, the shaykh's wife politely changed the topic of conversation.

Once the tribal women left, I asked Shaykha and Sharifa, who had just arrived, whether I could write down the names of members of their family. They were very willing because they were proud of the large size of their family.

Zayna, wife of one of Shaykh 'Abdalla's sons, then invited Amal and me to visit the house of her younger brother. I followed her along uneven and narrow alleys to another large house more in the center of the town. We entered a large, disorderly room whose floor was littered with nut shells. I can't recall the name of the nut, but it came from "the mountains" and was used for the hair. It was also edible, for one of the women ate some of the nuts that had fallen to the floor. The wife of Zayna's brother, a beautiful young woman with high cheekbones and a slender, aquiline nose, was reclining on a steel cot. She had given birth two weeks before to her fourth child, a son, who was nowhere in sight. We were served more food—oranges, bananas, chickpeas, pineapple, and a sweet, as well as many cups of coffee.

Several women entered the room while we were eating. To my surprise, one of them was Nasra, my next-door neighbor. She sat close to the woman who had given birth and spoke privately with her while I remained with Zayna and the older women who had been shelling nuts. Zayna brought a little dish with a yellow paste of saffron and water. She painted my forehead and Amal's, to my daughter's great delight.

Zayna then took Amal and me to a third house, that of Shaykh Ibrahim. By then I had had enough coffee and food. Amal needed a nap, but I did not know how to refuse. I found this third mud-brick house enormous. It was built on the edge of the town, full of light and spotlessly clean. On the second floor I was met by Shaykha, her mother, Sharifa, and one of Shaykha's six sisters. We drank coffee and ate chilled fruits that had just come out of a refrigerator. At one point in the conversation, someone asked me why I was wearing a light scarf on my head. "To cover my hair," I answered, puzzled by the question. "It is no good," someone said. Shayhka then brought me a *laysu*, the colorful printed shawl that every woman in Hamra wore when outside her house. I took the shawl, genuinely touched by the gift. Shaykha showed me how to place it on my head so that it covered my hair, neck, and shoulders. She and Sharifa then accompanied me, wearing the new laysu, and a truly tired Amal to my home.

On our way Sharifa laughingly told me that my husband might take a new wife since I had not given birth. I answered that a man could not take two wives at the same time in America. Shaykha, who did not yet have children, although she had been married for two years, nodded approvingly and said that she would not want her husband to take a second wife.

Many aspects of my first visits in Hamra perplexed me: the reaction to Amal in shaykhly households, the disorderly state of some houses where people of presumably high status lived, visiting patterns that I could not understand, and the presence in some households of a number of older women with unclear relations to the household. Were they servants or nannies? When I first visited Shaykh 'Abdalla's, a wrinkled old woman passed close behind me, and I naively asked whether she was the shaykh's mother. A hoot of laughter from a young girl nearby, immediately repressed, told me how wrong I was.

There were evidently some important status differences among people in the oasis. An obvious difference was that between shaykhs and nonshaykhs. Shakhly houses were much larger and tended to be conveniently located close to the head of the falaj where the cleanest water was available. Shaykhs could regularly entertain and feed large numbers of people. From the questions I was asked about Amal, they seemed to be more concerned about one's descent. However, these social differences could not be seen clearly in women's clothes, or even in general standards of living, which varied from house to house.

While talking to Nasra during my first weeks in Hamra, I learned of the social stigma attached to being the descendant of a slave.

> October 27. I though I heard some singing the day before. When I mentioned this to Nasra, whom I met washing dishes in the falaj, which was running in front of her doorstep that morning, she was curious but concluded that it must have been a radio. She told me that only women who are descendants of slaves sing. Even they sing only at night, during weddings. I asked her whether there would be any singing for the approaching Muslim holiday. She replied that men who were descendants of slaves would dance and beat drums in public, but that women and other men would just listen. "What do you

mean by khadim?" I asked. "Khuddam are just
like Indian [workers]," she replied. "They work
for you for a wage. They are often black, although some are not, but if a person is black, he
is certain to be a khadim. They are different
from poor people, because not all khuddam are
poor. Some are quite rich. They do not live with
you but are called in if someone is sick or if
there is a death in the family. They will take over
cooking, cleaning, and washing."

I then told her that some people were taking
my daughter, Amal, for the child of a khadima.
She stood up, quite taken aback, frowned, and
said sharply, "Who said such a thing? Who?
They are not good people who have said that."

I didn't answer her, of course. She did not
expect me to and went back to her washing. She
was silent for a few moments and then said in a
musing tone, as if talking to herself, "It must be
because of her hair . . . and her nose."

It was clear that Nasra also associated my daughter with a khadima, but it was also obvious that she
was angry that some people had told me so directly. It
seemed to her to be a breach of good manners and
hospitality. I think she guessed where I had heard the
term, but at the beginning of our stay, my nonshaykhly
neighbors discussed the shaykhly households with
great circumspection, at least in front of me, because
they were uncertain of my relationship with these
households.

Other social categories gradually became clear.

Some of the older women in shaykhly houses were described to me as "poor country women." Much later I learned that persons so described belonged to client (*mawla*) tribal groups of the 'Abriyin. The subtle social differences in practice between women of client status and the descendants of slaves remained unclear to me for a long time.

The logistics of maintaining a household took a great deal of my time during our first days in Hamra. We had a few hours of electricity each night from a wire connected to our landlord's electric generator, but during the first month of our stay we had no refrigerator (we eventually obtained a kerosene one). I was obliged to go to the market daily. Our house seemed to have some modern conveniences, but this was more appearance than reality. Water came when faucets were turned on and our new toilet flushed, but water was available in limited amounts only and was not potable. An uncovered cistern adjacent to our house filled up each time water ran in the falaj outside our door. Usually this was only once a week and less frequent later when water became scarce. Each evening, when we had electricity, we could pump the water into a smaller tank on the roof of our bedroom. Because there was so little water, I soon began using the falaj for washing my clothes, just as my neighbors did. It ran every other day. We also had to clean our house and courtyard of date pits, rusty nails, wood shavings, mouse droppings, and months of dust.

Our house teemed with reptile, mammal, and insect life. Lizards lived in the cracks of the ceiling and

Figure 3. "I soon began using the falaj for washing my clothes, just as my neighbors did."

came out to sun themselves. Frogs and toads croaked incessantly at night, especially near our water tank. Long columns of ants constantly crossed our courtyard, and chickens roamed freely in the adjacent orchard. They belonged to Zayna, who came every day to feed them leftover rice and sometimes to collect fruits from the orchards. A family of cats belonging to my nonshaykhly neighbors were attracted by the smell of my cooking. Vermin and all insects were unwelcome—the hordes of flies and mosquitoes, the huge spiders, the scorpions, snakes, mice, and rats.

I filled my first weeks in Hamra with hard physical work, worries, and the constant paradox of the unfamiliar. Many sights and sounds were initially exotic because they were all new and unfamiliar. I had to

learn a different set of gestures and new rules of etiquette. I had to establish a daily routine of some sort.
Images and sounds spun around in my head each
night, and the coffee I had to take each day did not
help me sleep. Children chanting Quranic verses, the
rhythmic sound of women grinding spices, donkeys
braying, invitations—"Miryam, come, come to drink
coffee"—small gifts of limes, garlic, and chips for
Amal left at our door when we were away, cats fighting in the night, mice scampering, the gentle swaying
of date palms in the moonlight, a young child running
past with a bottle of milk laced with coffee hanging
from her lips, dishes of fresh, juicy dates swarming
with flies, Badriyya rocking 'Abdalla, her infant
grandson, softly chanting the affectionate diminutive
of his name, "'Ubayd, 'Ubayd Allah."

In many parts of the Middle East and North Africa, most market activities are reserved for men;
women of higher status avoid the market completely.
In Hamra, no women ever went to the market. Being a
foreigner, and a more experienced shopper than my
husband in any case, I decided to ignore local practice
and shop on my own. One morning shortly after my
arrival I walked into the marketplace with a firm and
businesslike step. A group of men in white tunics
were standing in a circle around an auctioneer taking
bids for sheep and goats. The 'Id al-Kabīr, the feast
commemorating the sacrifice of Abraham, was barely
a month away. All households that can afford to do so
sacrifice an animal on this feast. It was a peak season
for the buying and selling of animals.

No one turned to look at me directly, but for a couple of seconds there was complete silence in the market, as if I were watching a market scene and the film had suddenly been cut. Then the quiet hum of voices of those engaged in the auction resumed. I searched for fresh fruits and vegetables and found a man with a pile of onions in front of him. "May I have two kilos, please," I asked. He replied incredulously, "You don't mean that you want these weighed, do you? There is no scale." I looked at his pile and told him that I could not carry home on foot such a large quantity. He finally agreed to sell me a small amount approximating two kilos. I entered the covered area of the market. Most shops were closed or were selling only basic tinned and dry goods. No fresh meat was sold on that day, but in one corner a man was cutting slices from a large fish that had been transported from the coast by truck. I bought a piece. Prices were fixed, and I heard no one bargaining. I circled the market again to make sure I had not missed anything and found an unattended, unopened carton that, on closer inspection, I found to contain oranges. "Are these for sale?" I asked an old man sitting farther away. "Where is the merchant? I want to buy some oranges." "He is out there," the man replied vaguely, without moving. After I repeated my request several times, he went to fetch the merchant, probably to get rid of me. When the owner of the oranges returned, he willingly sold me a dozen. He had been away buying fish for himself.

No one ever openly questioned my presence in

the marketplace. Soon I formed ties with a few merchants. I discovered that some of them had shops with
deep freezers, so that I could supplement the limited
quantities of fresh produce with frozen foods. Going
to the market every day was very time consuming for
me and my husband, who had to remain home with
Amal. We were both happy when our kerosene refrigerator finally arrived, delivered through the courtesy of my husband's sponsoring ministry.

The mainstay of Hamra's economic activities—
many men were wage earners elsewhere and returned
only on weekends—was irrigation agriculture supplemented by the herding of sheep and goats. One falaj
provided water for the entire oasis. Its water was distributed by a network of subsidiary canals to orchards
of dates and limes and small patches where other
crops grew. Beyond the oasis gardens there were
fields of alfalfa, sugar cane, sorghum, and some vegetables. These were irrigated by means of excess falaj
water in some years. At other times these fields were
irrigated by well water, almost exclusively drawn by
animal power (camels and oxen) until the late 1950s.
Since then animals have been progressively replaced
by motor pumps, which entirely replaced animal
power by the early 1970s.

Much of the locally grown produce—mangoes,
pomegranates, grapes, and bananas—never reached
the local market but were consumed by groups of related households. Except during a few months in late
winter, the only fresh vegetables to be found in the
Hamra market were onions and a green, leafy, spin-
achlike vegetable, and even these were not to be

found every day. Market activities were sporadic because they depended for the most part on unpredictable truck deliveries from larger cities. By midmorning, most stores in the market were already closed.

Two ways of handling commercial transactions existed side by side in the market. The older system involved men from Hamra and neighboring villages seasonally selling local produce by auction, with no weighing, little cash—small merchants almost never had change—and barter or exchange. A more recent way involved truck deliveries of goods, and fresh, tinned, and frozen foods previously unavailable in the oasis. There were fixed prices for these transactions.

After the initial round of invitations during our first week in Hamra, I was left more or less on my own. It was my turn to take the initiative. When I went for walks with Amal in the orchards and in town, women often invited us for coffee. I accepted invitations when people insisted, for everyone we met invited us out of politeness. But if I stayed home, no one called. One morning I stopped by unexpectedly at the house of my immediate neighbor. Nasra and Badriyya received me courteously, although I detected a movement of surprise on my arrival. I remained just long enough for a cup of coffee. The following day I visited again briefly in midafternoon. This time the two women appeared to expect my visit and greeted me warmly.

The pattern was set for frequent neighborly calls. Amal made friends with several of the children in the house who were her age. They quickly outgrew their initial fear of me. Soon I learned that a third woman lived in the household. She was Salma, the wife of Badriyya's eldest son. She had been away mourning her mother's death. The older women I had seen on my first visit were family members who helped take care of two of Salma's sons, three and five years old, whom she had left behind. She took with her only the youngest, six months old.

Salma and Nasra were women with contrasting personalities. Nasra was barely twenty years old. She loved to move, talk, tease, and laugh. Diminutive and wiry, she ran and sometimes leaped behind her goats to herd them home at nightfall. She enjoyed explaining to me some of her work—her sewing and machine embroidery, the types of dishes to be cooked for the coming holiday and the spices that were going to be used. She loved her two children passionately, painting their foreheads yellow with saffron, fumigating their clothes with incense, showering the youngest with kisses when few people were around. "I want at least ten children," she would tell me, smiling. A young Egyptian boy once hit her infant son. For the first and only time I found her visibly upset and controlling herself only with difficulty, mumbling under her breath and shaking her head.

Salma was older and more reserved. Nasra would shake with laughter at a joke; Salma would just smile. Her movements were measured, her words weighed. When I first met her, she was still mourning the recent death of her mother, a grief she did not overtly express except in her avoidance of face painting, perfume, and the wearing of elaborately embroidered pantaloons. Over the weeks the friendship that developed between one of her sons and my daughter drew us together considerably. Nonetheless, she remained a quiet, withdrawn person, conveying some of her feelings in small actions rather than words.

Both women appeared to get along with Badriyya, their mother-in-law, who helped them a great deal with their children. As the weeks passed, I was surprised at this continued harmony in the relations among the three women. There were no signs of strain, no looks of annoyance, frowns, or impatient words. Since some clash of wills seems inevitable in any society, there was obviously strong social pressure to avoid open or petty squabbling, at least when nonfamily members such as I were around. How did these women cope with conflict and disagreement?

Except for my brief business dealings at the market, I had little opportunity to meet and talk to men in Hamra. A handshake, a nod, a few words at the most, and they were gone. Women visitors avoided men in a household by leaving before men returned at midday or at nightfall.

The day was divided into periods when persons of the same sex, whether family members, neighbors, or acquaintances, could work and talk together. Other periods were strictly reserved for the coming together of close family members of both sexes in the household. In addition, in both shaykhly and nonshaykhly households, the husbands of many of the younger women worked out of town, either in the capital area or in Abu Dhabi, four hours away by an excellent paved road. These wage earners commuted back to Hamra once a week if they worked in the capital and usually once a month if they worked in Abu Dhabi. The result was that during the week there were many more young women than young men in the town. Among themselves, women in general spoke very little about men.

While I continued to be invited regularly for coffee by shaykhly women, I found more initial difficulty in building informal ties with them. Older women of high status seemed to be out visiting a great deal, and I often found no one home when I called unexpectedly at our landlord's house. A younger woman would run in from another part of the house and offer me the obligatory coffee and dates in the guest room; then off I would go, slightly puzzled that they seemed ill prepared for visitors if one called unexpectedly and disappointed not to have been invited to join in whatever the women were doing in the many rooms of the larger households. On my way to the market one morning, I met one of the wives of the paramount shaykh, accompanied by two other women. They were obviously visiting, but the reasons for, the frequency, and the pattern of these visits still escaped me. I tried exchanging lessons with one of the younger women. She was studying English at the local intermediate school, but the lessons soon stopped. The back rooms of our house, which our landlord had reserved for his grandsons, were used regularly by one of his wives, her daughter, and her daughter-in-law. They came in the afternoon to sit and peel dates to make a sweet (*halwa*), chatting informally and drinking coffee while they worked. I joined them regularly.

After a month these visits stopped. Shaykh 'Abdalla temporarily rented these rooms to an Egyptian schoolteacher, his wife, and their young son until a new apartment was completed for them in a small housing complex outside the oasis, which the shaykh owned and rented to the Ministry of Education for foreign schoolteachers. It was not a happy situation. Not only did it mean a loss of privacy—every word above a whisper carried from one part of the house to another—but I was afraid that we would be associated in people's minds with schoolteachers, and with Egyptians in particular, who were not always highly regarded because of their tendency to consider themselves vastly superior to Omanis.

Many women often failed to differentiate clearly between my accent in speaking Arabic and other Arabic dialects, especially Egyptian and Jordanian, with which they had equal difficulty. They lacked experience in dealing with non-Omani Arabs. The initial insistence by many oasis women of placing me and our Egyptian neighbors in the same category annoyed the Egyptians as well. Once a Hamra friend asked me whether I fasted. I said that I did not. Then she asked my Egyptian neighbor the same question. The Egyptian replied, "But I am a Muslim! She is a Christian!" She became even more upset when the Hamra woman, not quite understanding the Egyptian Arabic, then politely replied, "So you knew each other before you came to Hamra."

Islam as a way of life was so taken for granted by most men and women of the oasis that they did not think spontaneously in terms of categories such as Muslim and non-Muslim. Instead, there was a tendency to categorize persons in terms of those who practiced Islam versus those who lapsed in its practice. All foreigners, including Muslim Arabs, tended to be placed in the latter category. For many men and women in Hamra, the idea that my husband and I should live in the oasis and not be Muslims appeared incongruous. No foreigners, Muslim or non-Muslim, Arab or non-Arab, lived in the main part of the oasis itself. An older shaykhly woman shook with laughter one day at the thought that I would not fast during Ramadan, the Islamic month of fasting, so that I would be "just like an old woman." Earlier, when my husband visited the oasis alone and had to sleep overnight in the shaykh's sabla, he would be asked whether he was sick when he failed to get up and perform his predawn ablutions with everyone else. Once my presence became more familiar to the women of Hamra, those I got to know best put a gentle but persistent pressure on me to be more like them, to let my hair grow and part it like them in the middle, to learn to read the Quran (they were impressed that I could read Arabic), and to wear pantaloons under my skirts. It was even suggested that I should arrange for a reading of the Quran in honor of my daughter.

One month after our arrival, the oldest son of Shaykh Ibrahim unexpectedly died. This event changed my relationship with many person in the oasis. It separated me clearly from other foreigners who did not take part in the mourning. It drew me much closer to some of the shaykhly households with whom I then built informal ties. It also introduced me to a network of formal visiting that included women of all status in the oasis. I quickly began to learn about the meaning of family ties, forms of sociability, status differentiation, and how these were visible in modes of greetings, seating arrangements, and etiquette in serving food. I learned these as I took part in the long period of mourning and extensive visits that followed the death. I began to accompany shaykhly women on visiting rounds and to attend public readings of the Quran.

The death also changed my relations with my nonshaykhly neighbors. I continued to see them regularly, but now that they saw that I wished to participate in formal visiting, they began to let me know of births, deaths, and illnesses, and asked me to accompany them on their visiting rounds as well.

Soon my neighbors were regularly knocking at my door. When I answered, they quickly withdrew to the side to make sure that my husband did not see them while they waited for me. "Miryam, there is coffee at the house of so-and-so," they whispered, and off they went. I would pick up my head shawl, take my daughter by the hand, and follow them.

To some extent I had become part of the community. I remained an anomaly, a person with high status yet without relatives, one who was learned, a *mu'allima,* yet could not read the Quran properly, someone with poor Arabic and lacking experience in social matters, who did not fast and who wore "Turkish clothes" with no pantaloons under her skirts, a daring and slightly shocking habit in the Omani interior. But I was also known as a friendly person "who loves her daughter a great deal." Just before my departure, a shaykhly woman described me to a visitor as one "who visits us every day, eats our food, and perfumes herself just like us."

NOTES

1. The term shaykh is difficult to define because it has many partially overlapping meanings. It can be used to designate a religious scholar. A tribal leader is always addressed as shaykh as are other members of his lineage. Member of lineages formerly prominent will be addressed often by the term as will other individuals today wishing to challenge or lay claim to leadership of a tribe or a faction of it.

2.

THE HOUSEHOLD

ALMOST everyone in Hamra emphasizes the importance of the extended family, often speaking as if all households are large. Yet to my surprise I found that almost three-fourths of the households in Hamra are composed of "nuclear" families: a man, his wife, and children, or a widow or widower with sons and daughters. Some of these families include an elderly parent of either the husband or the wife.[1] There is a tendency for households related by kinship to be located near one another but nonetheless most remain small.

By speaking with many women I learned that the size of households varies considerably over time. Most men and women marry very young, usually in their teens, and for some girls by late childhood. The young husband frequently works as a migrant laborer, returning to Hamra weekly or once a month while his wife and later his small children remain in a larger household. This household is often the husband's father's house, though occasionally the couple lives with the wife's mother if she is a widow. In shaykhly households, the husband may be a student in the capital area or abroad. During our stay in Hamra, there was only one case of a man's moving into the house of his father-in-law after marriage. This practice is avoided because most people perceive the relation of father with son-in-law as an especially tense one if both men live under the same roof. Another common pattern is for two or three brothers or half-brothers, related through either father or mother, to share a household with their wives and children.

Considerations such as age, money, the nature of the husband's work and the availability of housing influence the decision to set up a new household. In recent years an additional consideration is the increasingly high cost of housing. Maintaining older mud-brick houses has become prohibitively expensive for many Omanis. Only a declining number of Omani craftsmen know the construction techniques involved. Moreover, space in the main part of Hamra is limited and many of its houses are inaccessible to motor vehicles. With money from emigrant labor, a growing number of households build cement houses on the periphery of the oasis, especially along the road connecting Hamra with the main Nizwa–'Ibri highway. The cost of constructing cement houses has rapidly increased because of the rising salaries of the Indian and Pakistani laborers who build them to the almost complete exclusion of previously available Omani labor (Birks and Sinclair, 1977b: 11).

Until recently, many shaykhly households were extended households. Sons of a shaykh tended to remain in their father's household for longer periods of time. In part this was because these houses were much larger than nonshaykhly ones. Hence there was sufficient space to accommodate several married sons, or even grandsons, and their families. Since the mid-1970s a handful of young shaykhly men have moved to the capital area with their families. If the wife has only very young children, the new household is not set up until another female relative, such as a widowed mother or an older sister of the husband, is found to live with her. An increasing number of the younger shaykhly generation are hoping to move into new housing in Hamra. Significantly, many of the new cement houses of extended family members continue to be built whenever possible within walking distance of one another, and close to the head of the falaj rather than on the periphery of the oasis.

The Organization of Domestic Work

Except for midday when men who work in Hamra return home to eat and to rest, the household is the domain of women and children from morning until sunset. Within its walls women do much of their work and they entertain many female guests, either formally or informally. Women are responsible for the smooth running of the household and they seek to ensure that their house is known for its hospitality. The household is also the area where family members meet in private.

Shaykhly and nonshaykhly households organize

domestic work in different ways, which I discuss here using examples of each. The differences reflect their respective ideas concerning work and money. My immediate neighbor, Nasir Sa'id, shares a house with his younger half-brother by a different father, Muhammad, and their elderly mother, Badriyya. Salma and Nasra, the wives of the two brothers, have a total of five children, four boys and one girl. The oldest of these is barely five years old. Nasir Sa'id is a soldier ('askari) attached to the staff of the governor in Hamra. His younger brother works the lands that they both own.

A few years ago the household moved from the main part of town. Convenience and better housing were the principal reasons for the move. The second house, shaded by a large mango tree, is much cooler than the other one. Most important of all, it is closer to one of the two main branches of the falaj. It is one of the older mud-brick houses, and in 1980 it still did not have electricity. Just before I left Hamra in 1981, the household joined with several nonshaykhly neighbors, bought shares in an electric generator, and had electric lights installed in their house.

Many household chores, including the washing of clothes and dishes, need to be done at the falaj. Nasra and Salma go to the stream three or four times daily, even more frequently in the summer, carrying large buckets of drinking water on their heads for themselves and their animals: one cow, four goats, some chickens and cats. One of their young children usually trails behind on these expeditions. Cooking meals and making bread is done every other day by both women. Nasra also tends the goats, taking them to nearby pasture just outside the orchards on winter mornings and driving them home in the evening. She collects forage during the summer months when few edible plants survive the heat outside the irrigated gardens.

Nasra and Salma are busiest in the summer. This is the season when dates and limes are harvested, dried, and prepared for storage. Both women sew by machine. They make all their clothes and many of their children's. Their husbands' tunics are made by a local Indian tailor because these require a zig-zag sewing machine, which the women do not own.

Badriyya, a grandmother, is nicknamed "the old one" (al-'ajūza) by her sons. She has trouble walking long distances but continues to perform an important share of daily chores. In addition to milking the cow and making yogurt at dawn every morning, she performs such sit-down tasks as peeling onions and hand-grinding coffee beans, grains, and spices with mortar and pestle. These duties require a great deal of strength. She is a substitute mother to Salma's three-year-old son, who finds it difficult to adjust to the fact that his mother is often nursing his youngest brother. She also cares for Salma's and Nasra's infant sons when their mothers go to the falaj or make formal visits to other households.

Salma and Nasra supplement the money that their husbands and parents give them by carrying on mini-businesses. Nasra sews women's clothes and machine-embroiders pantaloons and children's head caps.

Nasra's busiest periods are just before the two princi-pal Muslim feasts. The price for sewing each piece of clothing is fixed and quite low, given the time needed to do the work. Salma boils a batch of rose water every day. This is a lucrative enterprise that few women can afford to undertake because of the initial high capital investment. Dry rose petals are bought, washed, and simmered for an entire day over a wood fire. The rose water is then poured into small bottles. Salma sells a few bottles to neighbors who call on her. The rest are sold in the market by an *'arab,* or a nonrelated man, who keeps a share of the profit. Salma told me her profit was around double the amount originally in-vested for the dry rose petals. Nasra, hearing this, laughed and told me that Salma was a rich woman. Both women use the cash to buy clothes and little ex-tras such as sweets or plastic sandals for their children.

Another way some women make money is to sell various objects, such as pieces of precut cloth, pots, and children's clothes, at a small markup over the prices paid in the markets of Nizwa and Muscat. Ei-ther the woman herself buys a roll of cloth from an itinerant Baluchi merchant who comes periodically to Hamra, and then cuts the fabric into smaller sizes, or she has her husband or another related man buy her items unavailable in the Hamra market. She then re-sells them to other women locally. After the birth of a child there is a one-month visiting period called the *murabbiya,* during which time women giving birth of-ten display a few objects for sale. They are simply placed in the room where visiting takes place. Everyone knows the reason for the display, and there is no bargaining. Interested women make polite inquiries, and the transaction quietly takes place.

The Social Role of Water

In a country where water is scarce and running water was still unavailable, the falaj is essential to most household tasks. For most of the day the head of the falaj is reserved for women. Women make their ablutions here and pray in the courtyard of the small mosque adjoining the head of the falaj. Here they fill buckets with drinking water, which they carry home on their head.

Along the entire length of the falaj, women and young girls squat at its edge or stand in the half-foot-deep water throughout the day and early evening. They wash clothes, scrub pots, pans, and reed mats, and scrape the earth jars that keep drinking water cool with pebbles and water. Children bathe and splash in the water of the falaj for its entire length.

There are two main branches of the falaj. The *balād* branch (*sqiyit al-balād*) borders the edge of the main cluster of mud-brick houses in Hamra, called simply "the quarter" (*al-ḥāra*). It also defines one of the outermost edges of the gardens. The other branch, *sqiyit aṣ-Ṣaḥma*, defines the other limit of the gardens. It takes its name from a major mosque, used especially on feast days, built on its edge. Until the mid-1970s, housing was sparse along the edge of this

Figure 4.   Falaj and houses of 'Abriyin notables. A mjaza, a washing
house for women built over the falaj, is visible in the background. Photograph by Daryl Hill. Reprinted with permission from THE SULTANATE OF OMAN: A HERITAGE by
Ann and Daryl Hill. Longman, London & New York, 1977.

branch of the falaj. Now, with money from emigrant
labor, cement houses fill almost all the empty spaces
there used to be between the mud-brick houses.

Mosques, with adjacent washing houses for men (with cubicles for individual bathers inside) and washing houses for women, called *mjāzas*, alternate at intervals along the length of both branches of the falaj. There are seventeen in all, with a mosque at the head of the falaj and at the end of the two main branches. Shaykh 'Abdalla told my husband that mosques always define the limits of oases so that strangers—male—approaching the oasis for the first time would know without asking where to pray and make their ablutions.

I saw women of shaykhly status washing clothes along the falaj less often than other women. This was because they often used a mjaza or private bathing areas built into three of the shaykhly houses (and no others) that straddle the falaj. Several of the wealthier shaykhly families have recently bought electric pumps so that they can draw water at night, when the electric generator is running, from the falaj branches into roof tanks to provide their households with limited amounts of running water for private washing. Servant women from client tribal groups and the youngest girls of the households, those around ten years old, often do the heavier scrubbing for the shaykhly households.

The fetching of a bucket of drinking water from the head of the falaj is called *gharrafa,* a word that in classical Arabic means the scooping of enough water to be held in one's hand. At sunset, while some women pray, others stand in line and wait their turn to have access to clean water just as it emerges from underground. This is a time of day for handshaking, chatting, and joking among women of all statuses from various parts of the oasis. There is no hand kissing between shaykhly women and the descendants of slaves as there is on so many other occasions. During the ten minutes it takes to fill the last bucket of drinking water before the end of the day, status distinctions in Hamra are least conspicuous and the Ibadi ideal of equality comes closest to being realized.

The importance of the head of the falaj as a key meeting point for women of all statuses in the oasis is lessening. The small amount of rainfall in inner Oman in the last few years, and probably the declining standards of falaj maintenance (see Birks 1977b), caused the level of falaj water to drop dangerously low. In July 1980 the government set up ten small communal tanks for drinking water along the length of both branches of the falaj and supplied these with well water delivered by a tanker. As a consequence, women no longer had to go several times daily to the head of the falaj for drinking water.

A second element in the decline of the head of the falaj as a meeting point for women is the shifting spatial layout of the oasis. This is occurring as households invest in modern cement houses built outside the older, falaj-defined limits of the oasis. These households obtain their water from newly dug wells. In late 1982, when my husband returned to Hamra, he found that most women within walking distance of the head of the falaj still got water from it at least once a day, confirming its social significance. Water again became plentiful in 1982, but the pattern in which I participated of using the head of the falaj as the principal source for gathering water and meeting other women outside of formal visiting was decidedly in decline.

Work and Status

The lifestyle and work patterns of shaykhly women are similar to those of other women. Both engage in childcare, cooking, carrying drinking water, and washing clothes, although shaykhly women can perform some of these tasks more privately. Some shaykhly women also do some work in the orchards without impairing their status in any way. My shaykhly neighbor Zayna came daily to the family's orchard adjacent to our house to feed her chickens, collect eggs, gather limes and dry them, and dry dates (which have to be collected by men since only men can climb the date-palm trees) on the roof terrace of our shared house. In the same way I have seen all but men of the highest status work their land with pick and shovel side by side with their laborers in order to finish a task quickly; this is so because sufficient labor is no longer easy to find.

Several things set shaykhly women apart. They can openly have servants. They have markedly different attitudes than nonshaykhly women about buying and selling. They also go out visiting in the oasis much more often and receive many more guests.[2] I discuss the first two points in this chapter and reserve the issue of visiting patterns for later.

In wealthy shaykhly households, women retainers, both from client tribal groups and from descendants of slaves, do all the work in the orchards and some housework. In other households, shaykhly women work side by side with their servants. My immediate nonshaykhly neighbors, in contrast, can rely only on occasional help from one or two close neighbors and from some kin. When there is too much work, the women simply have to do with less sleep. Often during the winter I have seen them working next to the irrigation stream late in the evening by the light of a kerosene lantern.

Because of their high status, shaykhly women are barred from making pocket money through buying and selling in their own homes, or through preparing clothes, rose water, or other commodities for sale. It is not sewing itself or the making of rose water that is frowned upon. Shaykhly women do both. It is engaging in them for nonfamily members at a profit, no matter how nominal. Direct involvement in market activities is not prestigious. Indeed, only a few shaykhly men go in person to buy in the market. They usually engage retainers to do so on their behalf, and these men, usually descendants of slaves or Indian migrant laborers, are also entrusted with buying for certain shaykhly women. In 1980, 47 percent of the merchants in Hamra were of slave origin (Eickelman, 1980a: 8), although a large number of merchants had silent partnerships with shaykhs and other wealthier men who provided them with capital.

Fewer women today are willing to work for nonrelated households than was the case in the past, and even shaykhly households have difficulty engaging servants. Work in a nonrelated household publicly labels a man or woman as a client of the shaykhly household. Clientship implies explicit economic and social dependence. Migrant labor has freed many households, including those of descendants of slaves, from this form of dependence. For similar reasons few young men are willing to perform agricultural labor for others, even when they are paid high wages for doing so.

It is only during the visiting period after a birth or a death that women of slave origin enter nonshaykhly households to help with housework and serve coffee and fruits to female guests. For these services, they are paid a small wage in cash or kind, such as new clothes. Only men and women of slave origin engage in such tasks.

In his study of a South Arabian town, Bujra (1971: 45) mentions that *subyāns*, persons who once were attached to certain wealthy families, began working in the 1950s for anyone who was willing to pay. The younger generation of subyans, he continues, refuse to do this type of work and have taken up shopkeeping instead. A similar change is taking place in Hamra. Persons of slave origin who have been moderately successful in recent decades have deliberately loosened their ties with shaykhly households. Nonetheless, the social stigma of slave descent still exists, and many younger descendants of slaves continue to be clients of shaykhly households out of necessity. Relations between women of shaykhly descent and women of slave origin can often be tense, as will be seen later.

Two occupations are performed alike by shaykhly and nonshaykhly women. One is the teaching of the Quran to young girls. The other is the practice of traditional medical skills, including massages, medicinal branding, and midwifery. During my stay in Hamra, there were two female Quranic teachers. One, of nonshaykhly status, taught full-time and received a small stipend from the government for each child as well as a small customary fee from the parents. She also sold charms and amulets that were attached around children's necks to ward off evil. The other Quranic teacher with shaykhly status taught part-time only, and her students were shaykhly girls exclusively.

The distinction between the two teachers underscores the importance of whether payment is received for services. This is the case among both shaykhly women and nonshaykhly ones, but shaykhly women more assiduously avoid payment of all kinds. The question of payment is in all cases a delicate one and depends largely upon the relationship between the persons involved. If a midwife, for example, is a family member or a close neighbor, she is not paid. Women try to arrange for such services from people with whom they are close. Women of lower status are free to accept money and in fact expect a fee or gifts except from relatives and close neighbors. Thus my neighbor Rashida was midwife for the youngest children of Salma and Nasra. She was not paid. Nasra also received the gift of a charm for her infant son from the nonshaykhly Quranic teacher because the teacher was a relative. In contrast, a woman from a client tribal group whose massages were thought to cure infertile women worked for a fixed price for everyone.

Women of lower social status tend to be more active than those of higher status in moneymaking activities. In part this is out of necessity. Having less to lose, and possibly better understanding buying and selling because their husbands and fathers are more involved in these activities, they are freer to pursue economic gain. They sell more objects during the visiting period after childbirth. They can even engage in commerce in restricted contexts away from the marketplace. One leading merchant had a small shop adjacent to the tribal leader's house. Neighborhood women could buy directly from this shop because it was nearby and away from the main market. A non-shaykhly woman who lived a few houses away set up a rival mini-store in an old cabinet. She sold minute quantities of candy and cookies to neighboring children and had a small stock of cooking oil, detergents, and other basics. She sat at certain times of the day in front of her house, often with the cabinet closed. She assumed that everyone knew she was selling and would ask if they needed anything.

The women of the lowest status, the descendants of slaves, have a number of fairly distinct part-time economic activities in addition to serving at other houses. Some weave straw, making the fans used to brush flies away, brooms, and the head rings that enable women to carry heavy loads on their head. A few

older women also work nearly full-time as cloth peddlers, going from household to household with their
goods.

> February 22. Returning home this afternoon, I
> met Nasra and Rashida chatting on the path that
> runs between their houses. An old woman ap-
> proached with a bundle on her head. She was
> asked to open it. It contained some cloth, small
> packages of saffron, and little tubes of vaporizer.
> Nasra took one, sniffed it, placed it in her
> pocket, but did not pay the woman. Zayna, a
> neighbor whose house was farther along the
> path, passed by and looked interested. She was
> asked whether she wanted to see the cloth.
> "No," she answered, "not today, but come by
> tomorrow." She inquired about a special kind of
> cloth that the woman peddler did not have that
> day but said she would bring tomorrow.

> February 27. There was another woman selling
> cloth at Nasra's this morning. Rashida was also
> there with her coffee and dates. I am uncertain
> why the peddler was there, because no one was
> prepared to buy. She may have just been invited
> to chat, for she seemed on very good terms with
> Badriyya. Badriyya was tempted by one piece of
> cloth but returned it, saying that she did not
> have any money. The woman merchant insisted
> she take it anyway and pushed the cloth in
> her lap.

Women peddlers call by invitation only and expect the household that invites them to bring together a few persons, both relatives and neighbors, interested in their wares. There is never any bargaining. Payment is usually made at an agreed time later in the month. Coffee and dates are served after the buying and selling, making the occasion a distinctly social one. A similar pattern of discretion and avoidance of haggling over prices prevails in the men's marketplace.[3]

Women peddlers are a great source of delight and bearers of news from other parts of town. Their samples of cloth, precut pieces of synthetic fabric imported from India and Japan, are not very extensive but they can fill orders for other specific types of fabric. Often the woman peddler buys directly from the Nizwa market. Profit per piece does not appear to be very great, but peddlers seem to sell a fair amount. They also sell to women who come to Hamra periodically from the surrounding mountain villages and hamlets far away from the main roads, places where itinerant Baluchi peddlers never visit. Some of these countrywomen in turn sell the fabric in their own villages at a small profit, paying the town peddler once they receive payment themselves. If they are unsuccessful, they return the cloth to the town peddler.

Social Space

"Societies have generated their own rules, culturally determined, for making boundaries on the ground, and have divided the social into spheres, levels and territories with invisible fences and platforms to be scaled by abstract ladders and crossed by intangible bridges. . . ." (Ardener, 1981: 11–12.)

The passage I cite here comes from a preface to a collection of papers on social space. I cite it because it so excellently encapsulates what I came to realize of the central significance of how people use space to express and act out basic Omani notions of self and society. The separation of men and women for much of the day, the privacy of the household when family members are together, and hospitality to guests order how space is used in the household. This separation requires a careful coordination of movements on the part of household members in time and space, the implicit cooperation of other households, and careful attention to nonverbal cues indicating when a household desires privacy.

Figure 5 is a map of the house of my immediate neighbor, Nasir Sa'id.

The men's guest room (A) has a separate entrance and is never used by women. There are three small rooms used for sleeping and the storing of clothes, mattresses, and blankets. One is for Badriyya (C). The two others (D and E) are for her two sons and their respective families. The three women spend most of their time in the long, well-ventilated room (B), with windows opening into the orchards, or they sit on a mat under a mango tree in the courtyard. The roof of

A NONSHAYKHLY HOUSEHOLD

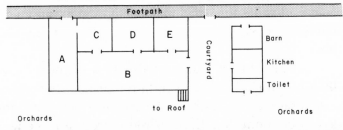

Figure 5. A nonshaykhly household.

the house is used for drying clothes, limes, and dates. Except on the coldest winter days, it is too hot to be used as a place to sit.

The segregation of the sexes within the household for much of the day facilitates visiting by nonrelated males and females. People simply will not call if they know that a husband and wife are together in the house because this relationship is considered a very private one that bars all but the closest family members. The presence of a man in the house prevents visits by unrelated women and vice versa. Except for a two-hour period in the middle of the day, the two brothers are usually not home in the daytime. When Muhammad is working in the orchards around his house, the outside gate is closed. Women take this as a cue and refrain from calling. Likewise, if the outside gate is open more widely than usual, neighbors know that the household is expecting a formal visit, usually of family members, and do not call. If a husband comes home from work earlier than expected and finds a woman visitor present, he retires into a side room and waits for her departure. Good manners decree that the woman will take her cue and cut her visit short.

Tact and the mutual coordination of movements allow the household to entertain guests of both sexes at separate times without feeling too cramped and also to be alone together. While there are in general more female guests than male ones in nonshaykhly households, nearly all households receive many male guests during the chief Islamic holidays, marriages, periods of mourning, and public readings of the Quran. When there is intense visiting by people of both sexes, such as for mournings, humble households spread mats outside a neighboring mosque or nearby communal guesthouse. Men use this space to receive guests and women use the house itself. Likewise, in households with no more than one room, guests cannot be entertained inside by either sex. In this case, women use a mat outside their house during the customary hours and men use a nearby communal guesthouse, of which there are several in Hamra.

The houses of shaykhly families tend to be much larger than those of most commoners. The additional space in these houses allows for guests of both sexes to be entertained separately at the same time. It also allows for private space for household members not occupied in receiving guests. There is much less need in these houses for a careful coordination of movement. Often small groups of women, usually of about the same age, gather separately.

Most of the large shaykhly households have been built along the main road parallel to the orchards and close to the head of the irrigation stream. Until 1970, there were only two Landrovers in the entire oasis, owned by two of its leading shaykhs, who widened the road in front of their houses to allow for the passage of vehicles.

Even visitors within Hamra sometimes find it difficult to know which door of a household to enter or, once she or he has passed the threshold, where to turn after that. Some households have two entrances, one to a men's guest room and a second one to the household proper. This second entrance is also used by female guests. In other large households there is only one entrance, and men and women immediately turn to separate sections of the house after passing the threshold. Many of the older shaykhly households have sections that were built at different times, when additional space was needed to house a second wife and her children or the wife and children of a son. As a consequence, the floor levels of various subsections are often highly uneven, making for even more confusion for visitors. In other households in which the first floor is used exclusively for storage, visitors must be guided to the barely visible stairway leading to the men's guest room and living quarters above. Once one enters an area reserved for guests, good manners oblige male and female guests to remain in their seats and not move to another part of the house unless invited.

Not all rooms are used in large shaykhly households. When cooking was done on wood fires, kitchens were located close to the roof terrace. Now that cooking gas is common, kitchens have shifted to rooms closer to the eating area. Some rooms are used only for parts of the year. I have seen a small cupboardlike and windowless room on the ground floor of a shaykhly house that a woman told me was used by herself, her husband, and their young children during the coldest months of the winter. In warmer weather, well-ventilated, larger rooms on the second floor are used. During the hottest months, nearly everyone in Hamra sleeps on roof terraces.[4]

Figure 6 is a diagram of the house of Shaykh Ibrahim. The shaykh's household includes his wife, like himself in her fifties, two unmarried daughters (Latifa, in her mid-thirties, and Fatima, about twenty-five), 'Azza, the widow of an older son who died while we were in Hamra, 'Azza's four children, a married son with his wife, Sharifa, and their small daughter. Shaykh Ibrahim has five other daughters, married and living in Hamra, one of whom moved to Muscat with her husband during our stay.

The house was built in the early 1960s, the last major mud-brick house to be constructed in Hamra. Compared to older homes, its plan is simple. The men's guest room (A) is immediately to the left as one enters and is slightly more elevated than the rest of the ground floor. Its windows overlook the main road rather than the interior courtyard—a feature absent from all but a few of the older shaykhly houses. From

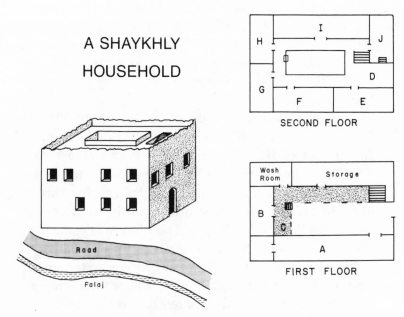

Figure 6. A shaykhly household.

his guest room, Shaykh Ibrahim can monitor all comings and goings in this part of town. Except for close family members, male visitors never get beyond the men's guest room. A small private room, actually an extension of the guest room, is reserved for confidential discussions. There is only one entrance to the house, but because the men's guest room is isolated from the rest of the house, both male and female guests can be received separately at the same time.

The remaining space on the ground floor is reserved for storage, cooking, and washing. Cooking is done in the roofed, half-open space (C on the map) next to the open courtyard. It is both shaded and well ventilated. Most cooking is done on a gas stove, but one of the shaykhly women in the house still makes bread over a wood fire.

Room B was used only twice during my stay in Hamra. It was set aside for mourning when the women first heard of the death of the shaykh's eldest son. They also took refuge in this room for an afternoon and evening during a violent sandstorm that threatened to break open the shutters on the windows of the upper floor of the house. The room was used after the first news of the son's death as an alternative to ushering guests to the customary rooms on the upper floor for receiving female guests, where formal hospitality had to be offered. Women of slave descent normally serve guests during mourning ('azā'), but on the first half-day the deceased was of such high status and the death so unexpected that the descendants of slaves mingled with everyone and mourned on an equal basis—an extraordinary circumstance which took place in a room normally unoccupied.

A stairway with high, irregular steps leads to where the women of the household receive visitors most often (D). It is not actually a room but part of the wide corridor that circles the open courtyard. A low railing is on one side of this corridor. From it the ground floor and courtyard are visible. The corridor is also open to daylight and gives a sense of openness often lacking in older housing. No matter what the time of day, a part of this corridor is always shaded and cool. Doors lead off the corridor to side rooms.

The areas of the second floor of the house are subject to different understandings of privacy. The entire second floor is accessible only to women and to close male relatives of the household, such as the shaykh, his sons, and the husbands of his daughters (all close relatives by descent). Some of its areas are used exclusively to receive female guests. Others are reserved for household members, and guests never enter them. For a woman to walk into a room uninvited and join a small private group of female household members would be considered a breach of courtesy.

Area D is the women's equivalent of the men's guest room. It is called *bayt al-'urubā*, which means literally "house of the foreigners." It is a public space where all female visitors are received. It is also used for informal coffee drinking among family members during visiting hours when guests might come by. Most female visitors never see any other rooms of the house. Few men, apart from those who live in the house, enter it. Husbands of the shaykh's daughters come here formally to greet their wives' mother when they arrive Thursday evenings for their "weekend," which lasts until Saturday morning.[5]

The shaykhly hostesses and their guests sit close to the walls. Persons of high status take seats near the windows that overlook the main street. These seats not only are the coolest in the room, they also allow the family members and preferred guests to observe, just like their male counterparts, movements on the main road. This vantage also gives persons of high status more control over the social situation. It gives them advance notice of who is about to visit. Although shaykhly women have very few social contacts with men outside their household, they are able to identify almost every driver by name or household.

The long, narrow rooms that surround the corridor are all considered private space. One room is for the shaykh's surviving son, who continues to live in his father's house, and for his wife and their young child. Another room is for the widow of the deceased son and her four children. These multipurpose rooms are used for sleeping, eating (food is carried upstairs by the small staircase in the back), and the informal gathering of family members. They are sparsely furnished—a carpet or reed mat on the floor and large wooden and metal trunks for storing clothes. Mattresses and blankets are kept in one corner. Shelves with serving trays, medicine bottles, and knickknacks line the walls. Rooms E and J are most commonly used by younger women and children to do homework, sew, and take care of little children because the activities of "main street" can be monitored at the same time.

The television set, a recent acquisition, is placed halfway between the public space reserved for women guests and the more private space of the bedroom-sitting rooms. At night television brings together young adults and school-age children as well as some older persons of each sex. Everyone listens avidly to the Egyptian soap operas. Some of the young children brought together by television viewing are potential marriage partners.

The Privacy of Meals

"It must be indelicate to eat in public. When the moment comes a sail is brought and arranged like a curtain around me." (Stark, 1940: 314.)[6]

As I mentioned earlier, guests discreetly leave before mealtimes in a household. Except on the very specific occasions discussed in this section, people rarely invite one another for meals. Nonfamily members are instead invited for coffee-drinking sessions, which can be quite elaborate and include a great deal of food. Every household in Hamra always has a thermos of coffee and a dish of dates ready for unexpected guests. However elaborate, coffee sessions are sharply distinguished from meals. In shaykhly and other houses where space is abundant, this perception is confirmed by the fact that coffee and whatever food is served with it are taken in the room where guests are received, whereas a meal (*ghadā'*)[7] is always eaten in one of the more private side rooms, even when guests are present.

In a large household such as Shaykh Ibrahim's, cooking is done communally for the entire household, but the food is then divided up to feed several groups of people. In smaller households men, women, and children usually eat together. These meals are infor-

mal, and there is considerable variation in eating patterns between households depending on individual
convenience and schedules. Eating is quick. I have
seen children in shaykhly households wolf down their
evening meal in less than five minutes and then rush
back to the television to avoid missing a popular Egyptian soap opera. Eating patterns bring out the family
subclusters that exist in larger households. For example, in polygynous households, the children, daughter-in-law, and grandchildren associated with the two
wives eat separately.

When out-of-town guests arrive in shaykhly
households—a regular occurrence—they are ushered
at mealtimes into a side room and eat either alone
there or with a person from the household. To honor a
guest, particularly a lower-ranking one, the host may
occasionally be present. If the guest is especially associated with one of the members of the household, the
bedroom of that person is more likely to be chosen for
eating. For example, on one of the Islamic feast days,
an Egyptian schoolteacher and I ate in the bedroom of
a young married woman who was also a student.

In the shaykhly houses, a similar pattern exists
for male guests. Shaykhs use their bedrooms occasionally to serve meals, and some bedrooms are furnished with this in mind. I once entered one with my
husband (ordinary rules of sexual segregation were
sometimes broken for us). It consisted of a long, narrow room with an elaborate, carved wooden bed,
probably imported from India, and a shelf of books at
one end. A Western-style couch and armchair stood at

another side, together with a table and chairs. Three
beautifully carved silver daggers attached to leather
belts, a submachine gun, and an ammunition belt
hung from pegs on the wall. Wall shelves were filled
with fancy china dishes, bottles of sweet orange drink,
perfume, and an incense burner. The floor was covered with carpets, and others were hung from the wall
or rolled up and placed on pegs to protect them from
mice. Stacks of grain were stored in a corner near the
door.

This tendency for guests to eat alone and apart
from the family cluster prevails in other Gulf communities. Hansen (1968: 158), who worked for four months
in a Shi'i village in Bahrain in 1960, noted the villagers'
reluctance to share a meal with her but attributed it to
a Shi'i unwillingness to eat with unbelievers. Having
eaten many times with Shi'i friends elsewhere in
Oman, I find her argument unconvincing. Hamra's
population is Ibadi, not Shi'i, but Ibadism is well-
known for its conservatism and has been accused, un-
justly in my judgment, of "fanaticism" and
xenophobia (see, for example, Barth, 1983: 53). I was
never stigmatized as an unbeliever, although I was the
only non-Muslim received regularly as a guest in the
oasis, and was treated in the same manner as other
guests. In part this is because, as mentioned earlier,
Islam is not thought of in contrast to other religious
traditions. It is so much a fabric of everyday life that
people do not think of categorizing strangers as Muslims or non-Muslims. Furthermore, this way of handling guests who are nonfamily members can more

readily be explained by an analysis of what is meant by propriety (*khajal*).[8]

The term khajal is hard to translate because it is so rich in contextual meanings. Dictionary translations include "shame," "bashfulness," "diffidence," and "timidity," but a closer gloss appropriate to inner Oman is "constraint caused by the fear of doing something improper;" hence my choice of the term "propriety." Khajal is a learned, stylized way of behaving that may or may not be accompanied by emotional feeling. Like the Javanese concept of "respect," incisively analyzed by Hildred Geertz (1959) in a discussion of the vocabulary of emotion, khajal is a cultural concept that becomes internalized in childhood and that presents to the individual a set of suggested cues on how to behave and how to order sensibilities. Khajal is a term used in a multitude of contexts. In leading a guest to a side room where a meal is waiting, the host or hostess often says, "Come and eat here so that you are not embarrassed" (fem., *la takhaj-jali*). If the person were left to eat in the guest area, he or she would be obliged for reasons of propriety to eat very little. If a shaykhly man enters an area of the household where his women kin are receiving guests, his presence triggers behavior on the part of all women present that is also called khajal. Eyes are lowered, backs become straight, and everyone is silent unless directly addressed. Women of low status visiting shaykhly households often maintain a stiff posture and answer only in monosyllables throughout their visit because of khajal. These are but a few examples of how khajal informs social life. Khajal frequently inhibits the range of possible social interaction and it is related to notions of status, a topic I will discuss later.

In the context of eating patterns, it can best be explained in the following way. Eating a meal, as opposed to drinking coffee, is considered to be a basic, almost a physiological activity. Relieving one's hunger is a private affair, like sleeping. It is to be done preferably in one's own household among close kin, or alone. The hostess, or host in the case of men, knows that it would be improper for a guest to eat to his or her heart's content in front of others. To avoid the embarrassment of wanting to eat but of being hampered from doing so by propriety, the guest is left to eat alone in a side room.

The private nature of the meal is also seen in the type of food eaten and how its serving contrasts with coffee drinking. Coffee drinking is the symbolic act the cements all ties, those of family cluster, neighbor, patron-client, and the fleeting one of offering hospitality to a stranger. To refuse to drink coffee with someone signals an active desire to cut existing ties with that person. If no prior ties exist, the refusal to drink coffee together implies that one or the other is unworthy of consideration. Coffee sessions can be elaborate in etiquette. In the more lavish ones, a sequence of dishes are offered that may include several courses of fruit and custard, chickpeas, and sweet vermicelli served in succession.[9]

A meal, on the other hand, always includes rice with meat or fish. Side dishes of sauce, salad, and limes might be offered as well. Bread is not essential, although it can serve as a substitute for rice. All the food is laid out at once, and there is little concern with procedure other than using one's right hand and taking food only from directly in front of oneself. A host or person of superior status will sometimes select choice morsels of meat and offer it to an honored guest. One can begin with meat or with rice, and do as one wishes. I found Omani meals in direct contrast with Moroccan ones because in Morocco the meal is not perceived as private in nature and a subtle etiquette prevails as to what is eaten first and how the food is eaten with one's fingers. In Oman, in contrast, one eats quickly and is not expected to talk much while eating. The ten or fifteen minutes that it takes for a guest to eat in private resembles a short rest during which he or she can relax and consume food without restraint. After washing, the guest then rejoins the hosts in the guest room for fruit and coffee and to take part in the polite general conversation.

The separation of guests from most household members at mealtimes also reflects the reluctance of both sexes to bring nonfamily members into household situations where they can share the intimate activities of the household, although occasionally this may occur.[10] Once during my stay in Hamra, my husband was traveling for six days to bedouin encampments. I was invited for lunch by my neighbors Nasra and Salma, to whom I had by then become close.

March 5. This morning I called on Salma and
Nasra. I gave them photographs I had taken of

themselves and their children, as well as some
knitting needles. They liked the pictures. When
they found out that my husband was still away,
they spontaneously invited me to stay for lunch.
We spent a pleasant morning chopping vegetables, plentiful just then and in season. We also
had to keep an eye on the children because they
got hold of my knitting needles and were wav-
ing them about enthusiastically. When the food
was ready, the women briefly hesitated over
whether they should give me a dish that I would
eat alone in my house. When I said that I preferred to eat with them, they immediately
agreed. First the children were served rice and
stewed vegetables (onions, tomatoes, and po-
tatoes cooked with the chicken). Then a large
dish of rice was prepared, with chopped ro-
maine lettuce placed on top. Badriyya carefully
divided the chicken. A portion went to all family
members, including the children, who had already eaten their rice. When the two husbands
returned, they could not eat with their wives, as
they normally did, because of my presence. So
they were sent rice and portions of chicken to
the guest room. They shouted back to their
wives that this was not the way to do things with
a guest and that all the meat should have been
placed on top of the rice, in order to allow the
guest to take as much as she wanted. Badriyya
apologized to me, saying there was only one
chicken and they were many. I agreed, and told

her that women knew better than men. They all nodded.

Their spontaneous invitation was generous. This informal sharing of a meal with household members is extremely rare in inner Oman. I took it as one of the warmest expressions of friendship I encountered during my stay in Hamra. The men remained in the guest room until I had left because this was the most polite way of dealing with my presence as a nonrelated woman. I knew them very little and am not sure they were overjoyed by this impromptu invitation on the part of their wives.

There are times when meals are eaten as a group with nonhousehold members, but these are all on well-defined social occasions that make everyday practice all the more clear by being in sharp contrast. These occasions include formal meals to make or seal agreements betwen groups of people. The most obvious occasion is the wedding breakfast, also called "lunch" (*ghada'*) despite its early hour of no later than six in the morning. Other occasions for a formal meal that occurred while we were in Hamra included a feast offered by a tribesman who wanted to secure the support of the shaykh for permission to dig a well, and the entertaining of guests of high status in the Ministry of the Interior and security services. Some formal meals are only for men; others, such as wedding breakfasts, include both men and women eating separately. These occasions are similar in that they are open only to specific individuals or groups, not to the entire community.

Other exceptions to everyday practice involve occasions that stress the unity of the entire community.
These include the two major feast days of the Muslim
calendar, the 'Id al-Fitr, the feast that occurs at the end
of the month of Ramadan, and the 'Id al-Kabir, or
Great Feast, for which every household that can afford
to do so sacrifices an animal. On these two major holidays, there is a dawn communal prayer at a nearby
promontory that serves as a communal prayer-ground
(maṣalla) at the edge of the oasis. Both men and
women attend, but the women sit apart and do not
participate in the public prayers. These feast days are
the only times of the year when women from the entire community gather outdoors, rather than in guest
rooms. On both of these occasions, there is also public
dancing and singing by men who are descendants of
slaves, and a communal roasting of sheep. A meal is
served in which all local officials and tribesmen participate, and much food is also taken home by poor
households. The men who do the cooking are mostly
descendants of slaves and persons from client tribal
groups, and they are paid from tribal funds for their
services.

Each of these feasts lasts for four days. For each
day there is a special dish served and all houses follow
the same progression of foods. On the first day, there
is a thick, porridgelike dish of ground corn and meat
('arīs); on the second day, a flat, pancakelike bread
and grilled meat; on the third day, roast meat and rice
(this is the day of the communal roast); and on the
fourth day, bread and sweets.

Finally, wealthier households occasionally organize a public recital of the Quran (*khatma*), for which an animal is sacrificed and a feast offered. Anyone who walks into a house is served a meal of rice and meat. Food may be served in the guest room—another

Figure 7. Woman watching 'Id celebration.

indication of the exceptional nature of these occa-sions.

March 15. Around 9 this morning, Rashida knocked at my door carrying a tray of spicy rice and chunks of boiled lamb. She said it came from Nasra's house and that I should come over to visit after I had finished eating. The gift sur-prised me. I joined them half an hour later. A group of women were busy cooking and wash-ing dishes. Nasra's mother was there and told me she had slept at her daughter's to help with the work that went on at night and early in the morning. Bashura, Salma's sister, was also pres-ent, as well as Rashida and several older women who often helped with the children. I was told that the occasion was a public reading of the Quran to thank God that the children were all well. "Who is reading the Quran?" I asked. I was surprised because earlier Quranic readings I had attended involved women only, not men as well, and never included a meal or the sacrifice of an animal. "The men are," Nasra answered. "Why didn't you tell me you were organizing this?" I asked Salma. I continued, "I spent the entire afternoon with you yesterday, and you didn't say a word about this, that you were plan-ning to stay up all night and cook." Salma smiled, pleased at my surprise. Leftovers of a large dish of rice and meat were next to her, as well as oranges and bananas. Nasra and Salma were busy dividing some of the rice with a little meat into smaller dishes, which Rashida then placed on a tray and carried on her head to distribute to neighbors. I counted six plates. Other women stirred two huge copper caldrons of boiling water and spices over wood fires. An enormous quantity of rice, some thirty pounds, was poured into the caldrons. I asked for whom this food was intended. Nasra told me that all their family (*ḥayyān*) were eating together this afternoon. We then sat down to have fruits, coffee, and sweets. Although the cooking was done at Nasra's, the eating was in the house of another relative.

As can be seen from the above description, public Quranic readings organized by individual households are lavish affairs. Not all Quranic readings are that elaborate and will be discussed later in greater detail in Chapter 6, dealing with formal visiting patterns among women. My point here is that Quranic readings are another occasion when eating rice and meat is no longer a private act to be done alone or with close household members. It is seen instead as an act of communion reinforcing ties among the wider network of family and neighbors. An earnest effort is also made to distribute food to as large a number of people as possible within the community in order to sustain one's reputation for hospitality and generosity.

NOTES

1. Of 354 households surveyed in detail by Eickelman (1980a: 12) 58 percent were composed of nuclear families. By adding

households containing an elderly parent of either the husband or wife to this figure, the proportion of nuclear households increases to 73 percent.

2. Compare Wright (1981: 136–157), who describes how influential women in an Iranian village were more constrained in their movements because they could only send other persons on errands. At the same time these Iranian women had more extensive contacts and wider social networks than other village women.

3. This pattern appears to be in sharp contrast to that described by Wikan (1982: 134) for Suhar, a large town on Oman's northern coast. Wikan claims that women swapped, bartered, and sold for cash a variety of items and tended to be "avaricious" in such sessions.

4. The practice of shifting room according to season used to exist in central Iran. In the Iranian case, rather than move up, the household moved in summers to a subterranean basement room (Bonine, 1980: 197).

5. The "weekend" in the Persian Gulf begins on Thursday afternoon and ends on Saturday morning. For soldiers and Ministry of Defence employees, the working week ends on Wednesday afternoon and resumes on Saturday morning.

6. When she made this comment, Freya Stark was a passenger on an Omani boat; hence the concern for her eating in privacy.

7. In classical Arabic the term means the midday meal. In inner Oman it refers to any occasion at which rice and meat are served, regardless of the hour.

8. Istiḥyāʾ is sometimes used by women as a synonym for khajal.

9. Wikan's (1982: 130) definition of a meal as "cooked food" as opposed to uncooked "snacks" does not apply to inner Oman, where certain food associated with coffee drinking, such as custard, sweet vermicelli, and a date dish (siḥḥ) are cooked. Sihh may even be served hot.

10. Wikan (1982: 133) gives an example of a woman eating meals with her husband separately from her parents when visiting her family. My guess is that the woman had married a nonkinsman, hence the separation between her husband and her parents at mealtime. Unfortunately, she does not elaborate.

3.

THE FAMILY CLUSTER

THE concept of family cluster (*ḥayyān*)[1] is crucial to understanding social life in inner Oman. Marriage choices, the formal and informal visiting patterns of both men and women, notions of public and private, the utilization of space within the household, and male-female relations are all closely linked with the notion of hayyan and the fundamental distinctions people make between family and nonfamily. Family clusters are perceived as forming mutually distinguished groups, each of which is bound together by socioeconomic ties and the sharing of information that is not revealed to others. In visiting patterns, women visit the households of hayyan much more often than other households, with the exception in some instances of a few close neighbors. Of more importance, the fact of hayyan relations affects how the visit takes place: the room in which they are received, the topics of conversation, the length of the visit and the occasion, and whether they remain for a meal. Topics such as the marriage of one's children and disagreements within the family cluster are never discussed in front of nonfamily members. Only within the family cluster may a woman sit and talk informally with men who are also its members, in the privacy of a member household, and with no nonfamily persons present.

There is no single term by which women label persons outside their family cluster. *Ajnabī* ("stranger") is sometimes used for persons living outside the oasis community, paralleling men's usage, which distinguishes between persons "from the land" (*min al-bilād* or *min al-waṭan*) or "from the community (*min aj-jamā'a*) and those who are not. The term *'arab* is occasionally used to label nonrelated men, especially of village origin, whether they live in Hamra or not. There is no term for nonrelated women except the negative one: "She is not from the family."

As women in Hamra use the term, there are two contextual meanings to hayyan. In formal usage, hayyan specifies a fairly well defined cluster of persons living in several households that are often adjacent to one another and commonly within walking distance. "If someone from my hayyan gives birth, I visit her house every day," several women said to me. Others have pointed out houses, instead of naming specific persons, implying that everyone living in the indicated house is hayyan. A woman expects other women of her family cluster to be at her side to receive visitors for twenty-five days after she gives birth or if there is a death in her household. Births, deaths, marriages, public readings of the Quran, and other occasions bring hayyan together. Women explicitly hope that their children will marry within the family cluster.

In informal, everyday usage, the term hayyan often refers to that component of the larger family cluster with which a woman has particularly close practical ties. Size is an important consideration, since a family cluster can vary from no more than two dozen to more than two hundred persons in the case of the dominant shaykhly lineage. "Sharifa has gone to visit her hayyan," a shaykhly woman once said to me, although both she and Sharifa belonged to the same formal family cluster. In this instance, she meant that Sharifa had gone to visit her father's household and that the people living in that household were her particularly close and intimate kin. A woman informally visits such close members of the family cluster frequently, often daily. She turns to them for protection or material help when necessary, and they often help with housework and childcare. A woman ideally forms her most intimate friendships with these close kin, although in practice this ideal is easier to realize among shaykhly women because their numbers and high status set them apart from their nonshaykhly neighbors.

The formal and everyday contexts of hayyan often are indistinguishable, especially if the family cluster is not large or if most of its members live in adjacent households. The two contextual meanings are most clearly distinguished for the shaykhly lineage and certain other large family clusters, in which case subclusters are more likely to form.

A woman's close hayyan are persons in her father's household, her mother, her sisters, including married ones who regularly visit her father's house, and brothers' wives if they are also kin and who may be living in her father's household. Marriage often means moving only a few households away. A married woman visits her parents' household at least several times a week. It is not unusual for a recently married woman in Hamra to spend up to half the day at her parents' house. If necessary, a married woman can seek protection and economic assistance from her father. Once he is incapacitated or deceased, she can turn to her brothers. One of my neighbors, Jukha, was a widow in her forties with a school-age son. She lived in a small house adjacent to that of her two brothers and their wives and children. A married daughter with two infants, whose husband worked as a truck driver in the capital area, also lived with her. If a woman's father and brothers are deceased, then her brothers' children can assume responsibility for her if necessary. I knew an elderly woman whose children had all died who went to live with her brother's children after her husband divorced her to marry a younger wife.

Family members with whom a woman is close and informal change over time. When she's young, a woman's social life focuses on her parents' house, although she will also see her married sisters and brothers' wives. With the death or disability of her parents, the maturing of her children, and increasing age, a woman's ties with her brothers' wives often become more formal. Visiting is frequently limited to marriages, births, deaths, sickness, and other family occasions. Informality and frequent visiting are reserved for the new generation of daughters, sons' wives, and granddaughters who now, in turn, come to visit the older woman's household. In that sense, a woman whose parents die before her own children are fully grown is socially less well off. My neighbor Salma was home in the afternoon much more often than her sister-in-law, Nasra. When I asked her why, she explained that Nasra was often at her parents' house, but that her father and mother were both dead. Another neighbor, Rashida, was in the same situation, although the fact that she had no children made her situation even worse.

> December 23. I asked Badriyya who are her hayyan. She began by naming her father, then her two brothers. She paused and then named her mother, her two sisters (still living in the nearby mountain village of Misfa, six kilometers away on a steep, winding road) and her brothers' children. "Is that all?" I asked. She hesitated, then gave me the names of her two husbands, both deceased. "Anyone else?" I asked. "The father of Salma is from my hayyan," she answered. "Salma's hayyan are mine." We spoke of Salma's immediate family. "How is her family linked with yours?" I asked. Badriyya answered that Salma's father shared a grandfather with her. "What is his name?" I asked. "Muhammad." Salma, who was listening to our conversation, interrupted us, smiled, and said softly, "Muhammad bin ["son of"] Sa'id. Sa'id bin Muhammad. Both are the same thing." I looked

puzzled, but she only repeated her words. I
then asked about Nasra. "Yes," Badriyya said,
"Nasra's hayyan are also ours. Nasra's father is a
child of a maternal uncle [khāl]," but she could
not give names. Actually, she hardly gave any
information on Nasra's family save the names of
her father and mother. Nasra has a half-sister
living in Nizwa and married to an office director
(mudīr), but Badriyya hesitated before calling her
a hayyan. "Far away," she said.

February 22. This afternoon I met Nasra, Salma,
and Rashida as they were starting on a visiting
round. They asked me to join them. On our way
to visiting a woman who had just given birth,
we passed by Nasra's and Salma's former house
in the center of town, now vacant most of the
time. Badriyya was in the house pounding corn,
the main ingredient of 'aris. Then we passed
Nasra's father's house next door. He was sitting
at his doorstep talking to a group of men. Her
mother was standing half-hidden in a corner,
probably waiting for us. We left Nasra's two-
year-old daughter with her. Salma's brother's
daughter lived in the next house. Across the
street, Salma's sister, who is the wife of one of
the Hamra shaykhs, greeted us from a window
and joined us for the visit.

Badriyya came to Hamra from Misfa some fifty
years ago. Like other migrants, her family sought to
settle in Hamra next to persons they could claim as

distantly related. Significantly, after Badriyya named for me the persons in her immediate hayyan cluster— her parents, brothers, sisters, and two deceased husbands—she began to name the households in Hamra with whom she had active ties and who had given wives to her two sons. She neglected to mention "close" kin in terms of descent who still lived in Misfa but whom she saw only infrequently. When I later asked her about these relatives, including her paternal and maternal uncles and aunts, she replied that they were all dead and that in any case she knew little about them.

In many nonshaykhly households such as Badriyya's, the exact kin relation of people who claim to be hayyan is imprecise or forgotten. Such households often are located side by side and represent themselves to outsiders as having close family bonds—a social fact often demonstrated by intermarriage among their children. Physical proximity is so important that people prefer to stretch the meaning of hayyan rather than marry their children outside the oasis community. As in most of the Middle East, descent is officially traced patrilineally. Indeed, women often name their fathers and brothers first when they are asked who are they hayyan. Nonetheless, the term hayyan includes bilateral relatives. It is applied flexibly to a wide range of kin, including paternal and maternal aunts and uncles, their children and grandchildren, half-brothers and half-sisters and their descendants, descendants of a joint grandfather, great-grandfather, and occasionally descendants of a common ancestor going back three or even four generations. The names of these ancestors are not important in themselves. In fact, they often alternate from generation to generation (e.g., Jabir ibn Muhsin ibn Jabir ibn Muhsin), making it difficult for even nonspecialist shaykhs to keep straight. What is important is that the family cluster asserts a strong sense of unity over time.[2]

Two things affects the size of the family cluster: physical proximity and status. Family members prefer to live whenever possible near one another in order to facilitate the formal and informal social visits expected of kin. Hayyan who do not live in the same town commute back and forth regularly in order to maintain active ties with their community of origin. This is the case among a few shaykhly families who have moved since the mid-1970s into houses and apartments in the capital area. If the hayyan relation remains dormant for a long period, it disappears. This is happening with Nasra's half-sister who lives in Nizwa. No visits were exchanged between the two sisters during my entire stay in Hamra, in part because of the difficulty of transportation, but also because the sister appears to have married someone of higher status who is not actively interested in maintaining links with her half-sister in Hamra. If the sisters (as they are usually referred to in Arabic without the qualification of "half") were living in the same community, they would see each other regardless of differences in status. Salma's youngest sister is second wife to a shaykh of the 'Abriyin. The difference in status between the husbands of the two sisters does not prevent them from seeing each other regularly.

The size of the hayyan cluster is reflected by its

status. This is seen clearly by the large gatherings in shaykhly households after a death, when all hayyan are obliged to make numerous visits. A corollary is that persons or households that are upwardly mobile try to build large hayyan clusters (especially through the households of cooperating brothers) or to emphasize the cohesion of their cluster by organizing, for example, lavish formal readings of the Quran. This practice also increases the tendency to include in the family cluster persons who are distant in terms of formal descent but who live in the same community.

One reason for the large size of the shaykhly lineage is the wealth and high status of some of the now-deceased shaykhs through whom present members of the shaykhly family cluster trace their interrelationships. There are practical benefits in terms of property and government recognition that are gained by asserting ties with the core of this shaykhly cluster. As a result, few persons allow their ties to the shaykhly family cluster to fall into disuse. Both young and old members of the shaykhly descent cluster show a great interest in genealogy and are knowledgeable in precisely how they are related to key persons in the shaykhly cluster. They can trace their descent farther back in time than can most members of nonshaykhly households. I did not meet even one woman from a shaykhly family who could not specifically pinpoint the exact kinship of her husband in relation to herself, even if this meant indicating relations through ancestors three or four generations removed from herself. In contrast, persons from nonshaykhly families often lacked specific kinship information beyond their grandfathers' generation. Even if they do have the information, they would not use it to augment their social status. They would simply be laughed at.

> January 9. One way of figuring out the existence of hayyan subclusters in shaykhly households is to observe when women begin wearing jewelry again after a death, or painting their foreheads with mahaleb or saffron. 'Azza's husband died two months ago. Nura, her sister, is not yet painting herself. Sharifa, another sister, is beginning to daub yellow dots on her young daughter but not on herself. He father's second wife and Zayna, wife of her half-brother, are painting themselves again.

Just as with nonshaykhly women, the core group of family members with whom a shaykhly woman has close informal daily contacts is not very large. If a shaykh has several wives, each wife, her daughters, daughters-in-law, and granddaughters form separate subclusters. If these women do not live in the same household, they are expected to see one another daily and to act as a group in many social contexts such as visiting together and sitting together at formal visits. Many details of daily life, such as how soon after a death a woman perfumes or paints herself, or the time and length of visiting during mournings, are indications of how women perceive their degree of closeness to other individuals within their larger hayyan cluster.

Privacy and the Family Cluster

The terms "private" and "public" have meanings specific to Oman. The distinction between the two terms ought not to be inferred from other cultural contexts. Anthropologists, especially those concerned with the Arab and Mediterranean worlds, are increasingly recognizing the culture-bound nature of notions of "public" and "private" and are expressing dissatisfaction with the generalization prevalent in much of the literature that the social world of women is private as opposed to the public social world of men (Nelson, 1974; Sciama, 1981; Joseph, 1983).

Privacy has a range of contextual meanings in Oman. The private sphere includes any activity or social occasion from which nonfamily members are excluded or any information that is shared by family members but kept secret from others. If, however, this information becomes known to other members of the community—a frequent and unavoidable occurrence in small, face-to-face communities—the information continues to be treated as private so long as everyone, both within the family cluster and outside of it, chooses not to discuss it in public.

One way of understanding the meaning of family in Oman is to look at the activities or occasions that are perceived as private to the family cluster, the types of information that are kept secret, the social mechanisms used to maintain privacy and secrecy, and when and how some events and information become public. In the previous chapter, I already discussed how people coordinate their movements to ensure privacy. Great care is also taken to maintain secrecy in planning or preparing for activities important to the family cluster, such as marriages and public readings of the Quran. Disputes within the family cluster and many personal problems are not discussed outside the family cluster. Women also hold as secret certain events, such as pregnancies.

One reason for secrecy is that it reduces the possibility of outside interference in the activities of the family cluster. It also lessens the effects of gossip if family disagreements or refusal in marriage negotiations become publicly known. Ideally, men and women within the family cluster try to hide all internal dissent and to present as smooth a front as possible to the rest of the community. In this, most family clusters are amazingly successful.

Simmel (1964: 335) describes the secret as something that "constantly receives and releases content: what originally was manifest becomes secret, and what once was hidden later sheds its concealment." He continues with the paradoxical idea that:

. . . under otherwise identical circumstances, human collective life requires a certain measure of secrecy which merely changes its topic: while leaving one of them, social life seizes upon another, and in all this alternation it preserves an unchanged quantity of secrecy. (Simmel, 1964: 335–336.)

Simmel's insight is useful in understanding secrecy in Oman. Some events become public only on the day they actually occur, such as the reading of the marriage contract (*mālka*), the birth of a child, the public recital of the Quran. Sometimes the best efforts to conceal family disputes from outsiders are unsuccessful. In the next chapter, I discuss the consequences if such disputes become public.

An essential mechanism for maintaining the privacy of the family cluster in inner Oman is what Simmel (1964: 321) calls "discretion" or "the staying away from the knowledge of all that the other does not expressly reveal to us." Persons in the community shy away from asking direct questions on matters perceived as private to the family cluster. Or if they discuss these matters, they do so obliquely through the use of a neutral third party, such as an adolescent girl, who cannot be held fully responsible for raising the matter. Discretion or tact also takes the form of a general avoidance by everyone of persons or situations seen as conflict-ridden. Confrontation is avoided whenever possible. People attempt to avoid conflicts within their own households for fear that these will culminate, if the conflict gets out of bounds, in the public disclosure of family problems. Disputes within the community are likewise averted whenever possible because open fighting detracts from the public image most persons seek to maintain of polite neutrality with the consequences, once again, of a loss of privacy.

Many of the qualities of the family cluster are not unique to Oman: the importance of physical proximity of component households, the elasticity and selectivity of what "family" means, the larger size of family clusters among high-status families, and the concern for privacy as a boundary-maintaining mechanism within the family cluster. These qualities help define family in many other Middle Eastern and Mediterranean societies. Likewise, secrecy usually plays an important role in small-town life and face-to-face communities elsewhere. What distinguishes Oman is the sharp lines of exclusiveness distinguishing the family cluster, the extreme care everyone takes to avoid open conflict within the family cluster and in the community, and the mixture of tact, civility, and circumspection with which family members neutralize their meetings with persons outside the family cluster. Family clusters seek to represent themselves as separate social islands, with members meeting others on prescribed social occasions only and then adhering to a strict code of civility that excludes topics likely to trigger contention. This image is obviously idealistic, but for some family clusters such as those of shaykhly lineage, it approximates reality because of its size and high status. Even among nonshaykhly family clusters, where family clusters are small and can maintain autonomy only with difficulty, women build close, informal ties with only a few select neighbors and kin.

Choosing a Spouse

Eickelman's (1980a: 17) social survey of Hamra indicates that 87 percent of Hamra marriages occur within the community (*jamā'a*). Of this number, 26 percent are to a person self-described as "close" kin, often a father's brother's daughter (*bint 'amm*) or a mother's brother's daughter (*bint khāl*). Unless persons are asked in detail, there is a tendency to self-describe bint khal marriages as bint 'amm marriages in order to bring actual practice more in conformity with the ideal of patrilineal descent groups. The remaining 61 percent of in-community marriages occur with "known" households of approximately the same social rank. A mere 13 percent of marriages are entered into with spouses outside the tribe or community.[3]

> December 1. "Why do you want to marry hay-yan?" I asked Nasra and Badriyya. "A woman likes to be near her relatives," Nasra answered. Badriyya added, "If a man mistreats her, she can return to her relatives easily."

To live near kin-related households has significant advantages for a woman. It gives her status, companionship, security, help in childcare, and protection from her husband or mother-in-law if a quarrel arises. I know several young women who reduced tensions with their husband's mother by spending large portions of their time with their own parents instead. In discussions with my husband, men in Hamra said that marriage is risky to someone from outside the family cluster or to someone of a different tribe. A father wants above all someone of good character for his daughter. A family member is the best choice because he is personally known and has the same public image to maintain. The bridewealth (*mahr*) is much smaller for marriages within the family cluster. Occasionally it is even merely token if two households have made an agreement to intermarry their sons and daughters. Economic factors alone compel many people to marry relatives. Marriage by equal exchange (*qiyāḍ*) is frequent in both shaykhly and nonshaykhly households. Before the 1950s there were a few marriages by qiyad among shaykhly families with shaykhs of different tribes for political reasons. With the cessation of tribal warfare and the diminished importance of tribal politics, marriage outside the tribe is now infrequent. Moreover, for shaykhly marriages outside the tribe, there were limitations to the extent that affinal relatives could participate in the hayyan cluster. If one's mother, for example, was from a different tribe, a hayyan relation was maintained with the mother's brothers and sisters (*akhwāl*) and with the first generation of their children (*arḥam*). Then the relation was dropped. Finally, a relative is preferred as a spouse because both men and women in shaykhly and nonshaykhly families are unwilling to break family bonds by allowing a woman to marry a "stranger." There is also an unwillingness to allow a "stranger," man or woman, to enter into the private realm of the family cluster. Men told my husband that such an in-law, even if of good character, would remain a "stranger" for life and be treated with the formality offered unrelated guests. For this reason, shaykhs prefer not to have their daughters marry if no suitable spouse is available within the family cluster, and some shaykhly women are remaining unmarried.

It is mostly persons of nonshaykhly status who

marry outside the family cluster or the community. There were high-status political marriages of shaykhly men and women outside the community in the past, but such marriages are rare today. In fact, I am aware of only one shaykh who has married outside his family cluster over the last decade. In that case, the woman was from a neighboring household and she became the shaykh's second wife. Descendants of ex-slaves tend to marry outside their family clusters and even outside the community, in part because of the small size of most of their family clusters. Bridewealth for "outside" marriages is much higher. Often such marriages are contracted by men who work in the capital area or in Abu Dhabi, because only these men earn wages high enough to amass the necessary funds. If anything goes wrong in a marriage between non-family members and becomes publicly known, such as a flagrant case of adultery (one such incident occurred during our stay in Hamra), then everyone agrees that the dereliction can partly be explained by the fact that the spouses do not share the same family cluster. There is an implicit assumption that the family cluster not only protects its men and women but that it effectively steers them away from improper behavior.

> March 9. "How did you get to marry your husband?" I asked Shamsiyya, whose husband is not of her family cluster. She blushed, visibly embarrassed, and answered, "My husband's sister was a wet nurse to someone in my family,

and I visited them when young. My husband
saw me and asked for me." She appeared so
uncomfortable that I changed the topic of conversation.

Shamsiyya came from the neighboring oasis of
Bahla and was now living with her young child in a
house shared by three brothers and their wives and
children. Her husband worked in Abu Dhabi and returned home monthly. The household was of nonshaykhly status but very well-to-do. Shamsiyya's
mother and other female relatives visited her regularly
in Hamra. Her confusion at my question was caused
in part because I had unintentionally asked her a very
private question. In Morocco, women would have
been delighted to answer my question. Besides, her
status in Hamra was precarious because, although she
had been in the oasis for six years, she arrived a
"stranger" and remained one in the eyes of most persons. Her one son had died in infancy, and her six-
month-old daughter was sickly. I noticed that each
time I visited the household, Shamsiyya's two sisters-
in-law emphasized, more so than did other households, how they all formed "one family." "All of us
are one," they kept repeating.

The milk tie as a bond facilitating marriage outside of the family cluster, or the community in this
case, deserves special mention. In a recent study of
elite urban women in Saudi Arabia, Altorki (1980:
233–244) shows how milk kinship, or the practice of
breastfeeding someone else's child and one's own at

the same time, served to broaden the network of kinsmen. As Altorki argues, milk ties in the past have been discussed largely in terms of how they prevent marriages between certain persons. This tie, however, can equally be used to broaden the number of "known" households and, as is the case in inner Oman, to broaden membership in the family cluster.

Formal announcement of the marriage contract often occurs at a very young age for both sexes and well before they are capable of establishing separate households. In Hamra I have met married girls as young as eight and married boys of eleven or twelve. Consummation is delayed until the physical maturity of the boy, but not necessarily for the girl. Several young women told me that they had not had their first period before their wedding night.

> February 20. At Shaykh Ibrahim's, Sharifa
> pointed to my daughter, Amal, then two years
> old, playing with her three-year-old nephew.
> She laughingly asked, "Will you marry Amal to
> Faysal?" I smiled, not answering yes or no, and
> then asked whether it was common to talk about
> marriage at such a young age. "Yes," she an-
> swered. "Women sometimes talk about marry-
> ing their children later, but such talk is not bind-
> ing and they are not obliged to marry."

All mothers whom I asked directly firmly denied having taken any part in the actual choosing of a spouse for their children or participating in the negotiations. Though formally the responsibility for choosing a spouse is solely the father's, the kind of half-joking conversation I had with Sharifa appears to be common among women who are friends. Since harmony among family members is highly prized, marriages are more easily negotiated between households whose women see one another regularly and who get along together. Altorki (1977: 277–287) shows how urban elite women in Saudi Arabia exercise power by having access to information on the prospective bride that is necessary so that men can make marriage decisions. When two houses are unrelated, this information is especially helpful. Although most marriages in Hamra are between households that are kin-related or that already have strong working ties with each other, the fact that a significant number of men spend a large amount of time outside the oasis makes women's visiting networks all the more important in arranging marriages.

It is difficult for children themselves to choose their own marriage partners when they are young. If a man is already mature, he will take a more active role in his choice of a spouse, although even in these cases the decision is effectively "framed" for him by members of his family cluster. Once a marriage choice is made, both shaykhly and nonshaykhly women agree that it is impossible for the prospective bride or the groom to contest their father's decision and openly refuse to marry. Men explained to my husband that the option of refusal was formally open to both men and women, but they admitted that such persons would need exceptionally strong wills and would be characterized as rebels if they objected.

Marriage Negotiations

October 15. I paid a brief visit to Nasra this afternoon. Our main topic of conversation was that Shaykh Ibrahim had taken one of his married daughters back home (*shālha*; literally, "he took her away"), although she had children and wished to remain with her husband. "Why?" I asked. At first Badriyya, who was with us, said that she did not know. Because I had only arrived in Hamra two weeks earlier, she was still uncertain about my relation with the shaykhly households. Then she volunteered that Shaykh Ibrahim was trying to marry another daughter, aged twenty-five, an old maid by Hamra's standards, into the same family cluster, and the shaykh was meeting resistance.

Marriage negotiations are kept very secret. In the Omani interior, they rarely involve the use of go-betweens from outside the family cluster. Only when something goes wrong in negotiations and becomes public knowledge, as was the case with Shaykh Ibrahim, do people discuss such affairs. Even then they do so discreetly among intimates, especially when the topic of discussion is a shaykhly household of much higher status. Shaykh Ibrahim's tactic evidently was unsuccessful; the married daughter returned to her husband some time later, and the older sister remained unmarried.

Public knowledge of pending negotiations is most unusual. It is more common to hear rumors concerning possible marriage partners, followed by vehement denials from the family of the women involved. These rumors are usually carried by the youngest women of the town, those in their teens or early twenties. When these young women discuss potential marriage partners, they usually joke and giggle, hiding behind their shawls, so as to evade responsibility for their words. Sometimes the marriages talked about take place; more often than not, no wedding takes place.

> February 21. I joined a group of young women, both married and unmarried, who sit every day in a shaded passageway off the main road, where they eat snacks and watch their children or younger brothers and sisters. There was some joking about 'Azza's being pregnant. She denied it, giggling and covering her face, saying that she was only sixteen. [In September I learned that she had indeed been pregnant.] There was also some joking about marriage. 'Aysha laughingly pointed at Thariya, a shaykhly girl about fourteen, and told me, "Thariya is to be married to Sultan bin Hamud, and her sister Fatima will marry Sultan's brother." Thariya vigorously denied this, saying to me, "Miryam, don't believe them. It is not true." More laughing and giggling.

Young girls in Hamra often first learn of marriage arrangement affecting them through the seemingly light and informal banter of neighbors and peers. Except for the firmness of her denial, Thariya did not appear to be particularly bothered. The young man in question is her maternal cousin, a possible marriage partner, and she had undoubtedly heard the gossip before. After all, Hamra is not a large oasis, and the range of appropriate spouses is limited. Even if she thought this rumor to be true, propriety required that she deny the possibility and refrain from engaging in speculation with her neighbors over so intimate a matter as marriage. Even in a household, propriety prevents a father from talking about marriage possibilities with his daughters. Mothers avoid the topic until they know that their daughter has learned the news from elsewhere. In part this is because of reluctance to speak about a potentially explosive topic; in part it is sorrow to see their daughters leave the household, even if they do remain within the community.

When I have asked young women what was their reaction on hearing the news that they were to be married, I received two different answers, the first describing an immediate reaction and the second depicting a more general notion of what one "should" feel.

"I cried a lot," said Muza, whose marriage contract was read when she was nine and whose marriage took place when she was twelve, "because I felt I was too young to get married." Muza, who was about sixteen when I met her, was then still without children.

She was attending intermediate school and spent more than half her time at her father's house. Because of this, her life after marriage showed no clear break with her life before. Just before I left Hamra, however, she was beginning to have serious problems with her husband's mother because she was not getting pregnant. "Girls are happy to hear they are getting married," said Nasra, talking in a more general way, "because all girls want to get married. Why? All women want children."

Taken together, Muza's and Nasra's statements reflect the mixed feelings of most young women at the time of their marriage. To some extent the contrast in their two statements is also due to the degree of satisfaction they have found in their particular marriage. The alternative of remaining unmarried is not a realistic or desirable one for them. It is only through marriage and children that a young girl's status is firmly secured. If she gives birth to many healthy sons, she can better her social position considerably.

Women often say that they had never seen their husbands before the wedding night (*zifaf*). This is an ideal that is not literally true in Hamra for most women. By the time marriage negotiations begin, most children or young people have probably been aware for quite some time who their possible marriage partners will be. They may have played with one another when they were younger. Since then they have had opportunities to catch glimpses at a distance of likely mates. When I pointed out to women that they must have seen their husband before marriage,

since so many marry relatives who live next door, they
replied that they had seen their future spouse, if at all,
only in the street and that once a marriage agreement
was signed, the young man and woman involved were
expected to avoid each other and refrain from visiting
in each other's household. This period of avoidance
lasts several years if the potential spouses are very
young. Girls who marry nonrelated men from outside
their immediate neighborhood or men from outside
the community often have no opportunity to know
their spouse before marriage.

The Marriage Contract

Wedding arrangements become public knowledge the
day of the reading of the marriage contract (*mālka*).
This usually takes place early in the morning, around
six, in order not to disrupt the day's work. Women do
not participate in the formal reciting, and in inner
Oman, no music, singing, or dancing accompanies
the event. After coffee and sweets, the men of the two
households have the tribal leader, judge, or other
qualified notable read the marriage contract. The essential elements in all marriage contracts, the only
ones specified by Islamic law, are the names of the
two parties and the amount of the bridewealth (mahr).
The groom kneels in front of the notable as the contract is read and repeats after him the words of the
contract in classical Arabic. The father or guardian of
the bride then comes in front of the notable. The con-

ditions of the contract are read to him. On behalf of the bride, he repeats the word to signal consent to the agreement.

> December 28. While going to the market, I noticed a crowd of people gathering in one house. I met Nasra's mother, who told me that they were celebrating the reading of a marriage contract. She led me into a room thick with the smoke of incense. Women filled the room. Some were sitting; some were standing because they were ready to leave; some carried large trays of fruits and bottles of perfumes. I recognized one shaykhly woman and asked her who was the bride. At first, she said she didn't know her name. This surprised me. Then she pointed to the bride's mother and told me her name. Nasra's mother returned and told me this was the house of one of her hayyan. She pointed out three or four houses next to one another and emphasized that they were all interrelated. Then she led me into a sideroom where a young girl of about fifteen was squatting, cutting up oranges for the guests. "This is the bride," she volunteered. The young girl, dressed in her ordinary clothes, looked up and smiled at me while continuing to work.

After the early-morning reading of the contract by the men, the women celebrate it separately later in the morning with a lavish coffee-drinking session with fruits, perfume, and incense. Family members and neighbors attend this celebration. The bride clearly plays only a passive role on the day of the contract reading. Since many marriages occur within the family cluster, the contract reading provides an occasion to reaffirm the existence of the group. Neither the bride nor the groom is a central figure then. The older woman who first invited me to the party for the contract reading repeatedly emphasized to me that the houses involved for the occasion all formed one family cluster. Her voice rang out loud and clear with pride as she spoke to me about the number of people present, because a large family cluster is associated with high status. Not until the birth of her first child does the bride herself become the center of attention.

Weddings

Contrasted with most other countries of the Middle East and North Africa, or even with coastal Oman, most weddings in the Omani interior are unostentatious and so little remarked by nonfamily members that it is difficult for an outsider like me even to know when one is taking place. In contrast to Morocco, where a wedding is an occasion for music and public display even in modest households, there were few public indications in Hamra. "Are there no women marrying right now?" I asked quite often. "Perhaps there is a special season for marriages?" No, people answered, there are weddings taking place, but we do not go to them. Since the bride is prepared for her wedding night and is taken to the groom's house in the evening, after sunset, a time when visiting outside the family cluster is rare, people are hesitant to invite a neighbor or a nonfamily member into the privacy of their household. The parents of the bride do not, of course, accompany their daughter to her new house, nor are they present at the wedding breakfast the next morning. The number of people attending most weddings is fairly small. Since I was earlier familiar with the lavishness, exuberance, and publicness of Moroccan weddings, the intimacy and sheer silence of weddings in inner Oman was astonishing to me. Nor is there any public display of blood to prove the bride's virginity. A young married woman told me that a bride would be too "embarrassed" (she used the verb *takhajali*) to have such an intimate part of herself shown in public. In any case, virginity is taken for granted because the bride is often so young and because the two households, especially if they are of the same family cluster, trust each other.

> November 27. I walked past the house of Nasra and Salma this afternoon and found their front door unusually wide open. I took the open door as an invitation to enter. In the kitchen, Badriyya and Salma smiled at me while stirring the contents of a large pot cooking on the gas stove. They were making sihh, a dish of cooked dates, butter, and black pepper. A few minutes later a group of women walked in. Nasra told me they

were Badriyya's hayyan. They included the two
wives of Badriyya's brothers and some younger
women, one of whom had a small child. The
formality of the visit surprised me. We sat on a
mat outside the house, with Badriyya and the
older woman sitting side by side and doing most
of the talking. Nasra sat a little apart, nursing
young 'Abdalla. Salma served. Hospitality was
lavish: the delicious hot date dish, coffee, oranges, tinned fruits, more coffee, sweet-
smelling ground spices that were powdered on
clothes, incense, saffron on the forehead and
cheeks, and perfumes. A few days later Nasra
explained to me that Salma's brother's daughter
had recently married Badriyya's brother's son;
hence the formal visit.

One month after the wedding there is a series of
visits by women living in the groom's household to all
other households considered to be part of their family
cluster. These visits are private in that no one outside
the family cluster is present unless, like me, they have
misread the cues and unintentionally stayed on. Privacy does not necessarily imply informality. Although
the women involved in the visit described above were
close kin and saw one another regularly, the reason
for the visit was perceived as a formal one. Everyone
was very reserved. The younger women let the older
ones do most of the talking. The subjects were general
ones, so that conversation could proceed gracefully.
The bride kept a low profile and said nothing. With-

out Nasra telling me who she was, I could not have guessed her identity.

Polygyny

A Muslim may legally have as many as four wives. I knew of no one in Hamra with four wives, although a small but significant number of men had two. The data collected for the 1980 Hamra Social Survey (Eickelman, 1980a) indicate that polygyny is most common among shaykhs and among descendants of slaves. The rate of polygyny is roughly three times higher for them than the rate found among the remaining non-shaykhly population. In the past some shaykhs took additional wives to cement political alliances with other tribal groups. Shaykhs remain under pressure to have as many sons as possible to maintain the numerical strength of their households. Women openly deplore the right of the husband to have several wives. Some married shaykhly women without children fear the possibility of a second wife, but they concede that if a man has no children by his first wife, he has no choice but to remarry. The higher rate of plural marriages among descendants of slaves is in part the result of well-paid jobs in the Gulf and in part an attempt to gain status by forming large family clusters.

Having children and bettering one's status are not the only reasons for taking a second wife. Some men never had children by their wives and never remar-

ried. Other men with several sons did so. Second
wives tend to be much younger than their husbands
and often, at least the few that I knew, were very
handsome. Obtaining an attractive, younger second
wife appears to be the reason behind some second
marriages and an added reason for women's hostility
to them.

Divorce is rare because of its repercussions upon
the complex, interlocking ties within the family cluster. In the case of a second marriage, the first wife
might remain in her husband's household. If the man
cannot afford to provide for two wives and there are
no children by the first marriage, the couple separates
and the first wife returns to live in the household of
her father, her brothers, or her brothers' children.
When the two wives remain and live under the same
roof, there is enormous pressure on them to appear to
live harmoniously regardless of their feelings. The
household's prestige is at stake if they quarrel openly.
If the household is a large one, as many shaykhly
houses tend to be, it is easy for the two wives to lead
separate lives outside of formal occasions. Even on
these occasions, co-wives never sit together. One or
more persons are always between them.

NOTES

1. Hayyan is a colloquial Omani term not found in classical
Arabic dictionaries. The closest classical term is *ḥayy*, which can
mean "organism," "tribe," or "quarter." In this account I use hayyan as it is used by both men and women in inner Oman. A more

formal term sometimes used by men is *qūrba*, the plural of *qarīb*, meaning literally "close ones."

2. In Morocco also, some families self-consciously construct a chain of alternating names, such as Muhammad bin 'Ali bin Muhammad bin 'Ali, to indicate partrilineal continuity. The restriction is that a son will be named only after a deceased ancestor. It would be considered an ill omen to name a child after a relative still alive. See Eickelman (1977: 48–50).

3. Marriage in Omani coastal communities follows a different pattern from that which I describe, and weddings are much more public. Wikan (1982: 189–211), who worked in the coastal town of Suhar in the mid-1970s, reports a tendency for marriages to be between persons not related who are neither neighbors nor members of the same community of origin. Barth (1983: 129), her husband, draws the same conclusion. Of a sample of 365 marriages, he writes that 14 percent have married "first and second cousins" and 86 percent have married "strangers." Unfortunately, Barth does not define "stranger," although he places the term in quotation marks. It is also unclear from his account whether Suharis perceive of family members as only those persons who are "first and second cousins" or whether it is Barth who has introduced this criterion to distinguish between "relatives" and "strangers." Nor do Barth and Wikan look at the meaning of intermediate terms, such as "community" (jama'a), which are essential to understanding marriage patterns. Hansen (1968), on the other hand, describes a pattern of marriages in a Shi'i village in Bahrain for the 1960s similar to that which I have described for inner Oman.

4.

SOCIABILITY

"A quarrel was a serious matter, as one could see by the anxiety of everyone to stop it." (Stark, 1936: 107.)

"During my whole stay on the island I never witnessed a single quarrel, nor anything that in the slightest degree approached even a dispute. The natives appeared to form one household, whose members were bound together by the ties of strong affection."
(Melville, 1983 [orig. 1846]: 240.)

Avoiding Conflict

The most striking characteristic of daily life in Oman, in contrast to many other Middle Eastern and Mediterranean societies, is the lack of open conflict and the pervasive civility and tact that mark all social conduct. In the preceding chapter, I have shown how oasis dwellers generally seek to avoid situations that they perceive as potentially leading to conflict. One of the highest compliments that can be said of a person is that he or she has the skill to avoid such situations. The consequences of open confrontation can be extremely serious. It can lead to physical assault or even homicide, although killing someone rarely occurs in contemporary Oman. Conflict within the family cluster is a matter of particular concern. Once a dispute within the family cluster becomes known to outsiders, the family cluster becomes a subject of gossip. The result is a loss of privacy and prestige for that particular family cluster.

> January 9. I was coming home from a murabbiya with a group of shaykhly women. On the path we met an old woman who was the mother of a man who had recently caught his wife with a lover. The man had gone to the governor *(wāli)*, who had both the lover and his wife sent to prison. The old woman conducted us to the nearby house where the scandal took place. As we climbed the stairs to the entrance of the house, there were little laughs from some of the shaykhly women in anticipation of the full version of the spicy story we were bound to hear. The family in question, descendants of slaves, were now fairly prosperous because the husband worked in Abu Dhabi. The shaykhly women inspected the house with great care, especially the terrace and the window into which the husband climbed at night to catch the lovers. There was a great deal of moving back and forth from one room to another. Women freely touched objects lying on shelves around the

room. Others even opened closed cardboard boxes. I was surprised at this conduct because it contrasted so radically with the propriety ordinarily shown during visits. After this inspection, we sat down to coffee and fruit while the husband's mother gave her version of the scandal.

In the above incident, the fact that the family involved was of low status precipitated the indiscreet behavior of the shaykhly women. In spite of the household's low status, the women would never have behaved with such a lack of restraint had the husband not made public his marital problems, in this case his wife's adultery, by involving the governor. This was the only case of adultery discovered during our stay in Hamra.

An obvious way to cope with conflict is to deny its existence on an abstract level in order to save the "face" of the community, the family cluster, or the household.

February 2. I asked Asila whether there were people in Hamra who sometimes were angry with one another and who did not visit. "No," she answered seriously. "Anger is bad [ma zayn], and no one does bad things here." Because I looked dubious, her sister, Fatima, acknowledged that some people do not visit one another because of bad feelings, but she did not elaborate.

Conflict is concealed so far as possible in order not to detract from the image of harmony that every meaningful social grouping seeks to present. Sharp words are rare; the raising of voices in anger is almost unknown. Asila herself was having serious disagreements with her daughter-in-law, Muza, who she was saying was infertile. Both women sought to conceal the tension between them, but it was quite evident, through small movements or comments when they were together, to friends who knew them both.

> March 11. When I visited Asila and some of her sisters, Muza came to greet us quite late, after having taken a nap. She looked unhappy. I was aware of a tension in the air between her and her mother-in-law. Muza did not shake hands, which she was not expected to do, but she was hardly smiling. The two women sat close to each other, the conduct expected of a mother and daughter-in-law, but Muza turned her body slightly away from Asila, a movement that could not fail to be noticed by others in the room.

When I returned to Hamra in the fall of 1980 after an absence of several months, Asila spoke openly with me about her attitude toward Muza. Following Hamra etiquette, I asked Asila for news of her daughter-in-law. She answered abruptly, "Muza is like you. She does not get pregnant." I made the appropriate comments about Muza's youth but felt sorry for the two women because of the unyielding attitudes they assumed toward each other. Asila was also obviously chiding me for having asked about Muza in the first place. She knew that I was aware of the tensions between them, and felt that I should not have asked for any "news" of Muza.

Fighting and marital problems are more likely to become public knowledge if a household is of low status. This is so in large part because the family clusters of which such households form a part lack the resources of personnel to protect them from scandal and to mediate conflict among themselves. They are more likely to have recourse to the governor, which members of a shaykhly cluster would never do, even in serious disputes.

> January 27. While I visited my neighbors for coffee this morning, there was talk of a woman, a descendant of a slave, whose husband beat her after he tried to have sex with her. She refused because she was having her period. She went to the governor, showed him the marks on her body, and asked that her husband be punished. The governor did not ask for corroboration. He ordered his soldiers to bring the husband and had him beaten on the soles of his feet with an iron rod. My neighbors concluded their discussion of the incident (which one of them learned about from her husband, who worked in the governor's office) by saying that the man was crazy.

> February 4. In my best gossipy form, I related the incident of wife beating to Asila and asked

her whether a shaykhly woman would have recourse to the governor if she was abused by her
husband. "Shaykhs do not beat their wives," she
answered sententiously. "That is only done by
the descendants of slaves. The governor will ask
the man to pay a fine to the woman of twenty
ryals [$60], or he will have him beaten on the
soles of his feet." "In other words," I replied, "if
a man is rich, he pays, and if he is poor, he gets
beaten." She laughed.

Here is an example of the most openly aggressive,
and therefore most highly atypical, conversation that I
had in Hamra.

February 29. A neighbor up the road just gave
birth. I went with Salma, Nasra, and the children to visit. Other neighbors were leaving as
we entered. We had barely sat down when some
seven or eight shaykhly women entered. There
was an immediate shuffling of persons to give
the best seats to the newcomers. I noticed that
Nasra, who had been sitting next to me, moved
very far away. Salma stayed in her corner with
two of her sons. I remained in my seat, and the
place next to mine was taken by Zayna, my
shaykhly neighbor. The atmosphere, which a
few moments ago had been informal and
friendly, became stiff and circumspect.
As I stood up to get my skirt incensed, some
women smiled because I was not wearing long
Omani pantaloons under my ankle-length skirt.
One shaykhly woman, in her forties, whom I did

not know well, looked at me sternly and asked, "Why don't you wear a tunic and pantaloons like us? It is forbidden [*ḥaram*] by the Quran not to wear pants." I maladroitly answered that she could not say it is haram because it is not written anywhere in the Quran. I asked her to show me the passage. "You are in Oman," she insisted, "and should wear Omani clothes," by which she meant the clothes worn by the women of Hamra. I was irritated by her tone and replied, "If you went to America, would you wear American clothes? Would you take off your head shawl and wear short skirts because this is what people wear?" The woman shook her head vigorously to indicate that she would not dress like that. I continued, "Because I am in Oman, I am wearing long skirts, long sleeves, and a head shawl. And that is enough." At this point Zayna made conciliatory comments on how beautiful my clothes were, and the matter was dropped.

After this exchange, very little was said, and the coffee session was perfunctory. I had barely selected a date when the dish was pulled away. No other fruits were served, but we were offered a very good sweet drink made from dates, followed quickly by perfume.

I was upset with the woman, not for criticizing my clothes, but for choosing to do so at a public gathering, something I had never heard done before. The shaykhly woman's annoyance was probably triggered not only by my clothes but by the fact that I, a person of high social rank in the oasis, was making visits in the community with nonshaykhly neighbors who sought to avoid being clients of the shaykhs and who were known to belong to a family cluster that was upwardly mobile. Attacking me, an outsider, was an indirect way of criticizing my nonshaykhly neighbors.

The reactions of the other women present in the room reflected the extreme uneasiness of people when faced with open conflict and the care they take not to become involved, even in witnessing the encounter. When the quarrel erupted, the incensing of guests' clothes was interrupted and everyone listened, motionless and passive. As soon as my anger became visible by my using a slightly louder voice and by the fact that I began to gesture as I spoke, Zayna, sitting next to me, whom I knew well, gave a signal for both of us to stop by praising my clothes. The fumigation of skirts and the serving of food to guest resumed, but our nonshaykhly hosts implicitly expressed their desire for this awkward visit to end as rapidly as possible by quickening the pace of hospitality. An unexpected consequence of this encounter was that Salma and Nasra, who were present in the room, in informal gatherings became more open with me about their own ambivalent feelings toward shaykhly households.

The most common means of curbing conflict is avoidance. I asked various women what they did if they got angry at their husbands. The almost invariable answer was, "I do not speak to him." I knew several young women who avoided their mothers-in-law

and spent most of their time at their parents' household instead, returning to their husbands' household
and their mothers-in-law only when their husbands
returned from Muscat for the weekend. Persons who
are not actually fighting but whose social position is
seen as potentially conflict-ridden avoid each other as
well. A man's co-wives eat and sleep in different parts
of the house, visit separately, and never sit next to one
another when propriety obliges them to attend the
same social occasion.

Another way of dealing with potentially tense situations is to let a third person, often an adolescent or
other immature person, communicate information of a
gossipy nature. In this way adults avoid assuming direct responsibility for the information conveyed. News
on who is pregnant, who has had a miscarriage, potential marriage partners, and who is being treated for
infertility is spread by girls or young women in this
manner.[1] Some of my unintentionally awkward questions (for example, when I asked questions of the traditional medical practitioner performing minor surgery on an infant) were answered by the youngest
persons present at the time instead of by the oldest as
would be so for less sensitive topics. My first questions about medicinal branding, a practice that most
women realize foreigners don't approve, were also
answered in this way.

> October 5. I was at a murabbiya at a shaykhly
> household. Zayna was perfuming my skirt with
> incense. I noticed a woman in a side room strug-

gling with a three-week-old infant. At first I
thought that she was trying to forcefeed the
child some medicine. The child was wailing.
This seemed to be such extraordinary behavior
that I stepped into the side room, the door of
which was ajar. To my dismay, I found that the
woman had a pair of nail clippers in her hands
and that she was cutting something in the child's
mouth. A few drops of blood dribbled out.
"What are you doing?" I asked as calmly as I
could. The woman smiled in an embarrassed
way. So did the mother, who was sitting at her
side, but neither woman answered me. I repeated my question. One of the younger women
in the room explained to me that she was cutting
the child's mouth so that the child would talk
properly. I still did not understand and asked
whether this was done for every child. "No,"
she continued, "only to children whose tongue
is attached by a membrane to the floor of the
mouth in such a way that he cannot stick his
tongue out. If this lower membrane is not cut,
the child will not talk well." By now the woman
had stopped cutting and was pouring olive oil
on the cut inside the mouth. The nail scissors
were on the carpet at her side. During this operation, except for acknowledging my presence,
the mother sat expressionless next to her child.
Finally, the child stopped crying and Nura, the
mother, took him in her arms and began to
anoint his forehead with saffron. The woman

who had operated on the child seemed unhappy at the results, mumbling that there was still some membrane left to be cut. Someone in the room asked no one in particular whether the child would be seen by a doctor, a question probably induced by my presence. No one answered. Either another attempt will be made to cut the child's membrane when the mother and the practitioner are alone, without a foreigner watching, or the child will be taken to a hospital for what appears to be very minor surgery.

I describe this incident in detail because it indicates the social context in which traditional medicine is practiced, a subject discussed later in greater detail. I introduce the subject here as an example of a social situation that was perceived as potentially very volatile. Since I was loosely associated with schools and hospitals, places where Omanis in the interior are most likely to come into contact with foreigners, it was expected that I would automatically criticize accepted local medicine.

I was assumed not to approve of what was going on. The strain was only somewhat eased by my effort to keep my questions as neutral as possible and to limit myself to knowing what was wrong with the child and what was being done. Once it became clear that I was not going to interrupt the operation, a third person, more disengaged than the mother and the medical practitioner, answered my questions. Since I was insisting on receiving an answer, someone had to respond to ensure that, as a guest, my feelings would not be hurt.

The behavior of the mother is worth noting. She sat rigid and impassive while her child screamed in pain and took great care not to display her own emotions. The dividing line between public and private comportment can be very thin. A guest who is not a member of the family cluster may show up at any time, and it would be most improper for such guests to witness an emotional outburst, even in the context of minor surgery. Once the operation was over, however, the mother took the child, rocked him, and painted his forehead with saffron—all signs of love.

Ideas of the Person

An individual's will is respected in principle. There appear to be few sanctions for doing wrong or for behaving differently from others, although such conduct rarely occurs. People do not reprimand others openly and indeed seek to avoid witnessing improper conduct. Joking, especially among younger women, silence, and looks of disapproval are the only sanctions I witnessed. In actuality, the very indirectness with which conflict is dealt with and the great care with which everyone tries to maintain a surface amiability magnify every small detail of social interaction and render it significant. The knowledge that every detail of sociability is scrutinized curtails the actions of individuals and obliges persons to conform just as effectively as more direct sanctions do. Not to visit certain households for a few days or not to sit next to certain persons is read immediately as a signal that something is amiss.

Within the limits circumscribed by propriety, individuals shy away from an open expression of their feelings. As is not so in other Middle Eastern countries, women's hands remain motionless in their laps while they converse and there is very little touching of other persons. The kissing of other adult women on the cheeks is rare.

> February 7. Karima, daughter of Shaykh Ibrahim, has moved to Muscat with her husband, her child, and an older unmarried sister of her husband. Three weeks after the move, she returned to Hamra for a brief visit. When the car carrying her showed up around 5 P.M., there was a stir of excitement in the guest room above where we were sitting. A few younger girls said the name of Karima's two-year-old son. He did not come with his mother. Because he was sick, he was left in Muscat with his aunt. When Karima entered the room, I was struck by the extreme formality of her greetings to her mother, sisters, and sisters-in-law. There was no kissing or hugging. Everyone stood up, and Karima formally went around the room, shaking hands, although I was the only outsider present. She then sat down and was served coffee, dates, and fruits like a guest of honor. Only then did the

formal etiquette relax. She began to talk about her apartment in Muscat, luxurious by Hamra standards, and about her aunt's visit to her in the city to see a dentist. By then it was close to sunset, the end of visiting time for neighbors; so I left.

March 11. "You do very little kissing," I said to a group of women at Shaykh Ibrahim's. "Why is that? Do you ever kiss your mother or your sisters?" Everyone laughed a great deal at my question. Someone replied that, as adults, they do not kiss others because people would laugh at them. Fatima volunteered that they might kiss the hand of their mother or their sister if they had not seen each other for a long time. I replied that they had not done so when their sister Karima came on a visit from Muscat. "True," she answered. "We don't do much kissing."

Both shaykhly and nonshaykhly women cope with emotional situations through formality. On some emotionally charged occasions, women's bodies will visibly stiffen in an attempt to speak the appropriate conventional words without showing personal feelings, whether the occasion is one of happiness or sadness at seeing a person leave. The rigidness of posture lasts for only a few minutes, just long enough for emotions to be checked. Then the atmosphere relaxes considerably. Self-control is also expected of a woman if her child dies soon after birth. After all, the life or death of a child is, like everything else, an expression of God's will. The woman continues to receive visitors as if nothing had happened.

In dress as in emotions, Omani women cover themselves completely at all times. Everyone always wears a head shawl except for a few younger women who allow it to slip from their heads to their shoulders at home. The public bath (*hammam*) so beloved by women in Morocco, which I have described to Omani women, is considered to be shocking, because it involves women seeing each other in a state of undress. Similarly, the wearing of a miniskirt under a black 'abaya, which I saw in Iraq and Iran in the late 1960s, is unthinkable in inner Oman. The laysu or thicker head shawl is never taken off on visits. Once when I was alone with Badriyya, I took off my head shawl to wrap it around my daughter, who was cold. Badriyya said nothing directly to me, but the sight of my bare head and my short-sleeved blouse, which the shawl had covered, made her so visibly uncomfortable that I was careful never to remove it again.

Clothes are an extension of the body, an observation also made by Wikan (1982: 106) and Kanafani (1983: 70), who describe how the face mask (*burqu'*) worn by women in the coastal areas of the Arab Gulf is simultaneously perceived as a beautifying device and as an integral part of a woman's self. In Hamra, clothes are washed daily, just as the body, and often at the same time. Men also wash their own clothes regularly. Subtle variations in clothes allow for some indirect expression of personal feelings. A woman who continues to mourn a loved one after the official mourning period ends can choose to wear simple, unadorned clothes. Head veils are often pulled over the face if a woman fears she will lose control of her emotions.

Personal feelings are often expressed obliquely through joking.

> October 19. Shaykha has been married for two years and Muza for a year and a half. Neither woman has children. Muza, aged fifteen, said that if she had no children by the time she was twenty, her husband would take a second wife. Shaykha, who was seventeen, laughed and agreed. All this was said in a light, joking manner, and I am not sure how to interpret it yet. "Has your husband told you this?" I asked Muza. "Yes," she answered, "but he was only joking." "Do you want children?" I asked them both. "Not yet," Muza answered, "but our husbands want them."

This exchange took place not long after I had arrived in Hamra. By the time I left, both women were being massaged regularly for infertility. Members of their family cluster persuaded them to have these treatments. Discussing the highly volatile matter of children in a humorous manner was the only way in which they could express concern for their infertility, an extremely serious condition in Hamra. Possible marriage partners, divorce, and pregnancy are other topics discussed in a similar manner.

Young women tend to talk of relations with their husbands in a joking manner that emphasizes sex. This is not because they perceive their ties to their husbands as primarily sexual in nature. Rather, it is because it is improper to talk in public about ties of friendship between a man and a woman even if they are husband and wife, although such ties often exist between spouses. Both propriety and the fear of joking, a form of social control, restrict discussion of the opposite sex and determine the style of these conversations.

A woman's status significantly affects her style of comportment. In shaykhly households, young women tease one another about their husbands. There were giggles when I was once shown the bedroom and Western-style bed of one of them. They joke about how happy some of them are on Thursday evenings when their husbands arrive from the capital. As women grow older, such joking ceases, principally because of the high social rank of many of the husbands and the perceived inappropriateness of these shaykhly men becoming the object of sexual joking.

Among nonshaykhly women, spontaneous and casual sexual joking is more likely to continue regardless of age, at least in informal coffee-drinking sessions among close neighbors. Some women of course feel more comfortable with such humor than others do.

January 30. I was sipping coffee with Jukha, her daughter, the wives of her two brothers, and

Nasra. Someone said that tomorrow was the
Prophet's birthday. Nasra laughingly said that all
of them were going to make love tonight, because it was a good night to conceive a child. She
said to me, "Tell your husband!" They all agreed
that they were going to be intimate with their
husbands that night, except for one woman
whose husband was away and another who said
her husband did not wish to make love to her
because she had no teeth. Everyone giggled.
Someone laughed and said that she could buy
false teeth in the Matrah market. Someone else
said that the irrigation canal would be dirty
tonight because everyone would be washing in it
after having made love. One woman then said
that she used the men's washhouse next to her
house together with her husband in the middle
of the night because no one else would be
around. Then she said to me, "You can use it
with your husband, too."

In the same way, shaykhly women behave in the
stylized manner induced by khajal in the presence
of their male relatives much more often than nonshaykhly women.

January 11. Shaykh Ibrahim walked into the
room where some of the women of his household and I were sitting. He sat down only a short
distance from us. As soon as he arrived, all
conversation stopped. Shawls were straight-

ened, tunics were pulled down, and backs were straightened. I was struck by this extreme reaction because, except for me, this was an informal gathering with only the shaykh's wife, his daughters, and one daughter-in-law present. He was in an unusually jovial mood and said things that made all the women laugh. When they did so, they tilted their heads to the side so as not to be looking directly at him and giggled nervously with their hands ready to cover their mouths. The shaykh told me I had a great deal of mercy to be raising an orphan. Then he encouraged us to sit in the sunlight where it was warmer and admonished a young girl whose head was uncovered, saying that it was too cold to go bareheaded. After drinking coffee, he left.

A similar reserve occurs when younger brothers and husbands pay brief courtesy calls on their aunts and female in-laws when they return from the capital. In these short meetings, the young men act as uncomfortable as the women. In contrast, nonshaykhly women do not appear demonstrably ill at ease if their husband, father, or a brother enters unexpectedly into the room where they are sitting. They exchange a few words with him, perhaps taking something he has brought them from the market. After a brief nod toward whatever women visitors happen to be present, the man takes his leave and sits in a side room until everyone leaves.

Women recognize these differences in styles of comportment, although they do not attribute them to

status. They simply say that some persons show khajal more often than others. This acknowledgment
does not imply that those who show more khajal are
somehow more respectable. Making jokes or simply
avoiding the issue may be used to achieve privacy or
propriety, or to dampen situations of potential conflict. A woman's status, her mood, and her perception
of the particular social situation all play a role in determining how she behaves.[2]

A sense of trust in the predictable comportment
of others in the community is a reassuring aspect of
oasis life. Once I asked Nasra whether she had told
her husband where we were going to visit. She shook
her head negatively. Then she smiled and added, "He
knows," meaning that he knew that she was making
one of her regular social calls and that he trusted her.
When Asila told me in a deadpan way that no one did
bad things in Hamra, she was alluding to the wide-
spread sense of trust that is an essential part of community life in inner Oman.

Oasis society is characterized by marked social
inequality and serious tensions among some categories of people. Nonetheless, these internal divisions
are overridden by the shared perception that the people of Hamra form part of one tribe and one community, separate from others. It is the reason why my
neighbors merely pushed a bolt through their door
before leaving their homes, a token way of preventing
intrusions since anyone could push the door open. A
shared sense of community is also manifested in the
continued existence of women's formal visiting networks. This sense of trust in the comportment of oth-

ers in the community gives women considerable freedom within the oasis—freedom to organize their
workday and their visiting as they see fit. Paradox-
ically, the people of Hamra place a high value on individual responsibility and noninterference in the affairs
of others. At the same time, the range of comportment
in public, and even within the household and family
cluster, is sharply limited by a strict code of conduct
that everyone is assumed to know and accept. The
consequent necessity for indirectness in dealing with
others magnifies the most minute details of social interaction.

NOTES

1. A similar role may be played by young men. See Gilsenan
(1982: 120–23) for the ways young men in a Lebanese village share
information on male-female relations and marriage.

2. For a discussion of the stylized communication between
some Afghani men and women when they meet in public, see
Anderson (1982).

5.

NEIGHBORS

NOT all neighbors are kin. Some unrelated neighbors form close bonds of friendship and visit one another as close family members. Nonetheless, most of the inhabitants of Hamra say that developing close ties with unrelated neighbors is decidedly less desirable than the ideal of forming close ties within the family cluster alone. Badriyya felt the need to justify, at least to me, Rashida's frequent informal visiting.

"Rashida comes to visit us often because she has no children and few family members. Her parents are dead, and she has just one brother. Her husband's parents are also dead, and he has one brother who does not live with them."

The role of neighbor is ambiguous. They can be helpful and even indispensable when help or advice is needed and no family member lives close by. They are potential kin since marriage into a "known" household is very important. Yet neighborly ties are precarious because their initial base is solely physical propinquity. Once a household moves away, a phenomenon increasingly common in the post-1970 era, women cease to maintain informal visiting ties with former neighbors. In addition, while women who are neighbors try to maintain friendly relations with one another, opportunities for quarrels abound. Finally, not all neighboring households are equal in status. Although slight differences in status can be set aside in some social contexts, the informality and implicit equality expected in interaction among neighbors can be extremely difficult to maintain if status distinctions are too pronounced.

Shaykhly women are rarely informal with persons outside their family cluster because of their high status and the fact that a large number of shaykhly households are situated close to one another. Non-shaykhly persons who are immediate neighbors of shaykhly households tend to adopt active client ties, performing informal services for the shaykhly households and in turn receiving assistance of one form or another. The maintenance of client ties, just as those of family cluster and neighbor, takes the form of daily visiting and coffee drinking. Some women of client status make formal visiting rounds with their shaykhly neighbors. However, persons who are not clients of shaykhly households are in an awkward position. They do not make joint visits with their shaykhly neighbors lest they compromise themselves as being of client status. Because of my own anomalous role in Hamra, I was the only person there who after a few weeks could informally visit shaykhly houses on an equal footing without being myself of shaykhly descent.

During the winter some adolescents and young married women of shaykhly descent sit daily in a narrow side path with other young neighbors, some of whom are daughters of clients. Together they watch over younger brothers and sisters. This kind of informal sitting together ceases when they are older. It is significant that the informal setting of these gatherings and the youth of the participants lead to antagonisms being very thinly disguised.

> December 8. I was sitting with the group of young girls and married women babysitting in a side passageway when Ibtisama arrived, carrying her youngest child. She is a young woman of slave descent. On seeing me, she joined the group. One young woman turned to me and asked, "Miryam, who has the prettiest child? This woman [she pointed to Ibtisama, who is clearly of African origin] or this woman [she pointed to a young shaykhly woman with a very white-skinned child of about the same age]?" "What a question!" I answered. "All babies are beautiful." My answer pleased Ibtisama so much that she turned to me with a grin of triumph and invited me for coffee at her house. I accepted and walked away with Ibtisama amid dead silence.

February 4. I met again with the circle of young women who were caring for the small children in the passageway. Someone had prepared a dish of *marsa,* a liquid sauce similar to salad dressing into which green onions were dipped after folding over the stem several times. The green onions were first presented in a dish, but there was so much laughing, joking, and pushing to get at the sauce that the green onions soon scattered all over the ground. Tharaya, a young girl of shaykhly descent, turned toward me and said, "I don't like green onions," and she refused to eat from the dish. Ibtisama came along just then and greeted me cheerfully. She made room for herself within the circle and began to eat, complaining that there was dirt in the onions, which indeed there was. Tharaya and another young girl said nothing, but they frowned slightly at Ibtisama. Again silence.

The second incident is interesting for the oblique manner in which these women expressed their status consciousness and sense of disapproval. Tharaya may not have cared for green onions, but she was also separating herself from what she perceived as extremely poor and unshaykhly manners. She was also furious at Ibtisama for joining the group in such an open and aggressive manner, using her tie with me, and for her criticism of the food, which implied indirectly that she, Tharaya, or someone else in the group was capable of preparing and eating dirty food. Yet disapproval of her was expressed by no more than a muted glance.

Figure 8. "During the winter, some adolescents and young married women of shaykhly descent sit daily in a narrow side path with other young neighbors. . . ." Photograph by Birgitte Grue.

Clusters

Here I want briefly to sketch the ties that Salma and Nasra have with their neighbors in order to pinpoint more precisely the distinctive characteristics of such ties and show how people cope with subtle differences in status. Rashida is in her thirties and childless. Her husband works locally for one of the ministries. They live at the edge of the orchard in a mudbrick house. As a midwife, Rashida assisted in the births of Salma's and Nasra's youngest children. I often saw her cradling the infants in her arms while the two mothers saw to household tasks. She helps Salma wash rose petals in the falaj. Because Salma and Nasra have a larger and busier household, Rashida visits them more often than Salma and Nasra visit her. The three women often go together on formal visits to people not related to them. By the end of my stay in Hamra, the two households were sharing the use of an electric generator that provided them with light in the evening. When Rashida's husband goes out in the evening, she spends the time at Nasra's and Salma's in order not to be alone. In fact, she is the only example of which I am aware of a nonrelated woman visiting a household during the evening when husband and wife are together.

Jukha, another neighbor, came to Hamra with her husband and child from a neighboring village about fifteen years ago. A widow and quite poor, she lives with her married daughter, her daughter's children, and a young son in a small house next to the road that borders the orchard. Adjacent to her house are those of her two brothers and their families. Jukha comes during the summer months to help Nasra and Salma dry dates and limes. During the winter Nasra's four goats pasture next to Jukha's house, and Jukha keeps an eye on the animals. Nasra and Badriyya sometimes give her money and gifts of fruit for her services, but payment is always discreet and the women never describe their relationship in terms of work. A friendship has developed among Nasra, Jukha, Jukha's daughter, and Jukha's two sisters-in-law. During the cool winter months Nasra often brings a thermos of coffee and a dish of dates to Jukha's house and shares them with the four women, who sit on a mat in front of the house. One of Jukha's sisters-in-law had a year-old mentally retarded child who was in poor health. Nasra helped the woman see someone to have the child branded, a form of traditional medicine that is still used for serious illness in Omani villages. Despite their close ties, Jukha never makes formal visits in the community with Nasra because of their differences in status.

A few weeks after my arrival in Hamra, I became an accepted member of the visiting group of Nasra, Salma, and Rashida. Nasra's and Salma's children played together constantly with my daughter, and this served to draw us together. An Egyptian woman who lived behind our house with her husband and child for a few weeks also visited Salma and Nasra regularly, although she did not accompany us on visiting rounds in the community. Significantly, Salma and Nasra do not have informal neighborly ties with the shaykhly women who used the part of our house adjacent to our own before the arrival of the Egyptian family and after their departure. Visiting shaykhly households occurs only on formal occasions, such as births, deaths, and serious illnesses.

No one explicitly calls their neighbors "friends," although it is clear that some neighbors develop close ties of friendship. Neighbors instead describe their relationships with one another in terms of need—a need for companionship, for example, on the part of Rashida, who has no children and little family. When I once asked Nasra why she was visiting Jukha as often as every afternoon at one point, she answered unconvincingly that she went to sun herself. Nasra's courtyard was indeed shaded and cool in the winter. What she did not want to say, or could not, was that perhaps she was enjoying the company of these neighbors more than she did that of her sister-in-law, Salma, who tended to be withdrawn. One must provide a specific reason for visiting neighbors at least when an outsider like me asks; this is not the case for members of one's own family cluster.

Neighborly ties extend only to households immediately next to one another so that, while there is some overlap, clusters of neighbors are fairly distinct. A woman cannot choose to build close ties with a neighbor farther up the road, skipping the women of households closer to her own house. Wikan (1982: 139) notes a similar pattern for the coastal town of Suhar. Neighborliness is based strictly on residential proximity rather than on "personal evaluations," although there is some room for maneuver. Not all women of a household visit their neighbors with equal frequency. Thus Salma visited Jukha much less often than did Nasra.

February 8. This afternoon, a Friday, an older woman who is related to Rashida came to visit at Nasra's. She was full of news about people I did not know. Another neighbor, who lives farther up the road, dropped in for coffee and then quickly left, carrying a bottle of rose water she bought from Salma. No money was exchanged. Nasra then asked me if I would join her on a visit to Jukha's. I accepted, and Badriyya said that she might join us later. Badriyya's legs were hurting. So she limited her visits to necessary ones. After Nasra had left, I asked Salma why she never seemed to accompany us to Jukha's. She gave a quiet, embarrassed laugh and did not answer. I asked again a little later, and she answered that she wasn't angry at Jukha but that she had visited her yesterday. [This was not the case. I had seen Nasra returning home alone from Jukha's the day before.] She then said to me, "Take Sa'id [her eight-month-old son]. Go to Jukha's with him. I will join you later." I took the child, who made no protest because I had often held him, and I went. Salma never joined us. When I returned an hour later, I found her sewing.

My question placed Salma in a dilemma, compelling her to answer me at least in a roundabout way. On the one hand, it was a serious matter to say in Hamra that a certain house was "not visited." Such a statement would be interpreted as anger or open fighting between the households, a situation that people seek to avoid at all costs. Salma's immediate response was to assure me that she was not angry at Jukha. On the other hand, Salma may have been seeking to avoid Nasra, or she may have felt that there was too much status difference between herself and Jukha to visit often. She may simply have preferred to be alone for a few hours every day. This would have been another reason that would not be confided to anyone else. Since Salma and I were close and our children played together frequently, she decided to give me the care of her youngest son for an hour, a sign of great trust in Oman, so that I would not be hurt by her oblique answer to my question, and to have the child visit Jukha in her place. I never found out exactly why Salma appeared to avoid these afternoon visits to Jukha. Afterward, perhaps as a direct result of my unintentionally awkward question, she joined us more often.

Salma and Nasra had some latitude in determining who were their neighbors because their house was in the orchards, where housing is dispersed. In one direction, their house is separated from the next house by several small fields, so that it is beyond seeing and hearing range. For months, women of the two households limited their interaction to cordial greetings when they passed one another along the narrow orchard paths. Finally, just before my departure from Hamra, they exchanged visits to which Rashida and I were also invited. The food offered was elaborate since the two households did not know each other well and the atmosphere was one of cordial formality. In private, I asked Nasra several times why these exchanges took place, and she denied there was any reason beyond ordinary hospitality. I left the oasis shortly after these visits, and so I never learned the reasons behind them. Still, these visits show how people can manipulate and redefine the boundaries of neighborhood clusters. One possible reason for the decision of the two houses to initiate closer ties was the fact that both were fairly prosperous and non-shaykhly in status.

A neighbor making an unexpected arrival usually brings a thermos of coffee and a dish of dates with her. The gesture implies that no special preparation need be made for her. Once a visit begins, one or two other neighbors, including me, may be called in to participate if they are known to have informal ties with the household. The coffee and dates brought by the guest are first served, followed by those of the host household. Conversation is extremely relaxed when women know one another well and there are no wide discrepancies of status. Some days there is a great deal of joking, often about husbands and sex. Occasionally the invitation is for a specific purpose, such as visiting someone who is sick or meeting a woman who sells cloth.

February 26. I went to my neighbors so that
Amal could play with their children. I was
greeted warmly. After coffee and dates, Nasra
and Salma said that they were going to Jukha's.
She was ill with an abscess on her thigh. We
took along a thermos of coffee and some dates.
Jukha's daughter was there as usual, and the
wives of Jukha's two brothers joined us. Then
Rashida arrived with her coffee and dates, followed by 'Asima and her mother, women of a
client tribal group who lived next door to Jukha,
and three other neighbors from houses farther
up the road. This was an unusually large neighborly gathering because Jukha was ailing.
Seating was informal, but Jukha was at the center. At least five different dishes of dates were
offered with coffee. The dates were first served
to Badriyya and to 'Asima's mother because they
were the oldest. There was a lot of joking about
a neighbor who was taking a second wife and
about the amount of the bridewealth. Just then
the man was working only a few yards away,
constructing an extra room for a house. There
was additional whispering and giggling at the
thought that he might have heard what was being said. One neighbor talked to Nasra about
her child, who had just been branded. We also
talked about clothes, perhaps because the
women were expecting the Baluchi cloth merchant to drive by soon. The coffee-drinking
session ended when the Baluchi's truck arrived
and the women stopped him on the road so they

could look at his fabrics. The women marveled at the colors as they touched the bright, synthetic fabrics. 'Asima bought a roll of cloth, which she intends to cut up and sell piecemeal. There was no bargaining, and she paid the merchant immediately in cash.

March 12. Around 4:30 P.M., Salma, Nasra, and Rashida knocked lightly at my door and invited me to join them on a visit to a neighboring woman who had just been hit by a car earlier that day in Bahla. We found the elderly woman lying down with a heavy blanket over her in spite of the heat. It was unclear what was wrong with her. Soon other women arrived and filled up the room. Dates and a sesame dip were offered with the coffee, and juice was brought out for the children. Incense was burned and perfume was offered. So the condition of the injured woman must not have been very serious. Some small bottles of perfume for sale were passed around and were sniffed a great deal, although no one bought any. We talked mostly about the accident.

March 14. I went to Rashida's for coffee with Nasra, Salma, and Badriyya, as well as one of their older relatives who is deaf. It was my first time in Rashida's house. Of course we brought dates and a thermos of coffee with us. Then we had Rashida's coffee, dates, and tinned pineapple. Rashida burned various kinds of incense. I had a cold and was told to breathe some of the smoke deeply. Afterward we painted ourselves with saffron diluted with a little water. I was given too much saffron and asked Nasra what to do with the rest, which was in my hand. She said, "Wipe it on your clothes so that you smell good when you sleep with your husband tonight."

Gossip

There is often an undercurrent of gossip in conversation among close neighbors. Gossip has the attractiveness of the forbidden, for in gossip a woman comes close to invading the privacy of another person or another family cluster. When it occurs, it takes place only among those few neighbors who can be trusted not to repeat conversations and reinforces the intimacy of social ties.

> February 23. The talk this morning as I was sipping coffee with Rashida, Salma, Nasra, and Badriyya concerned the high cement wall that was being built around our garden. I did not know the reasons for building the wall, but one of the shaykh's wives once complained to me that Salma's child ate fruits off their trees—something I had never seen the child do. Yesterday Zayna showed me her chicken coop behind our house and complained that she was no

longer finding eggs in it. "Do you know what
has happened to the eggs?" she asked me.
"No," I answered, "but I will try to see if anyone
comes into the garden." I mentioned Zayna's
problem to my neighbors this morning, and
there were exclamations from all the women
present. "How could you know about her eggs?"
Badriyya said. "Besides," Nasra added sar-
castically, "doesn't she know that chickens
change home from time to time? We don't know
about her eggs, and you don't, either." Badriyya
complained that in the past their hens laid eggs
in Zayna's garden. They lost the eggs and could
do nothing about it. Conversation then turned to
Shaykh Ibrahim's daughters and how old were
the two that were still unmarried. Badriyya
could give approximations in relation to when
other people were born, but not in years. I was
asked whether Zayna's sons ever used the rooms
behind our house. "No, no one is there at
night," I answered, "but Zayna comes in the
afternoon to make rose water and to sew with
her husband's mother." Everyone was interested, and Rashida added, "Yes, she has two
sewing machines in there."

March 5. I saw Zayna and a woman helper from
a client tribal group walking around Rashida's
garden this evening. After they left, I talked to
Rashida over the wall between our houses. She
told me that Zayna had been looking for her

eggs and had found that her chickens had been laying their eggs in her [Rashida's] garden. Rashida laughed. There was no egg thief after all.

The tenor of Salma's and Nasra's relations with their shaykhly neighbors was ambivalent. It encompassed a mixture of curiosity, grudging recognition of superior status, caution, and censure. They were fascinated by events in shaykhly households but weighed their words carefully when speaking unless in the company of trusted persons. In such company, they lost their reserve and voiced criticism of shaykhly actions. In fact, the only persons I heard criticized were persons of shaykhly status, which I took to be an indication of social distance. For the most part, these criticisms were oblique, usually no more than a brief exclamation at some turn of events or a curt statement followed by a brief silence. In a discussion of neighborly gatherings in an Iranian village, Wright (1981: 150) describes a similar caution among women who avoided direct comments, whether favorable or unfavorable, in discussing households with which they had direct and frequent social relations. It was only in talking about a more distant part of the village or another settlement that comments were, though only slightly, more direct. In a similar way, the high status of shaykhly persons made them socially distant from the nonshaykhly population and thus more vulnerable to discreet criticism and gossip. At the same time, their high rank was acknowledged and envied. When

Badriyya once fell ill, Salma and Nasra were very pleased at an unexpected visit from their shaykhly neighbors. The promptness with which they told me of the visit and their tone of voice made their pleasure clear.

6.
THE COMMUNITY

". . . it is charming to see the women come in and greet the company assembled on the floor: they do not straighten themselves between one greeting and the next, but walk gracefully in a stooping position from hand to hand as it reaches up to them, trailing their gowns among the teacups which, like small coracles in the wake of a steamer, have to do the best they can. If the person to be greeted happens to be absorbed in conversation, the newcomer, still stooping, snaps her fingers as noisily as she can to draw attention, and having obtained her hand-kiss, moves on. The ceremony goes all around the room, until the circle of the slaves is reached."

(Stark, 1940: 37–38.)

FREYA STARK traveled in the Hadhramaut in the 1930s and provides one of the few accounts by European visitors to the Arabian peninsula that recognize the importance of women's visiting networks. In inner Oman, women's tunics are shorter and do not trail and there is no finger snapping or hand kissing, but at any formal gathering of women there is the same slow ritual of going around the room and greeting

everyone individually, the same circles of descendants of slaves clearly distinguished from the freeborn, and, for women of lesser status, the same stooping from hand to hand. This practice of handshaking
everyone individually is prevalent at gatherings of
men or women in many parts of the Middle East and
North Africa.

Seating order is important at these gatherings
because it is a public statement of status. One side of
the room, usually by the windows, is reserved for
women of higher status, such as the elderly women of
shaykhly families. Other people are seated in de-
scending order on either side of the women of highest
status. Age and early arrival affect seating to a certain
extent, but there are implicit rules that result in a re-
shuffling of seating order as new persons arrive. A
person of slave origin or client status, for example, no
matter how old, never sits directly next to a shaykhly
woman in a formal gathering.

Even foreigners are assimilated into local orders
of precedence. In the finely calibrated seating patterns
prevalent in men's formal gatherings, my husband
was invariably seated next to the tribal shaykh but
ahead of the shaykh's brother, or just after the shaykh
and the provincial governor. If police or army officers
were present, for seating purposes he was ranked
above captain but below colonel. On his return to
Oman in 1982 after an absence of nearly two years, his
status was slightly elevated.

There is never any rushing to a specific seat or
area. Women seem to know immediately where to ori-

ent themselves. Guests who are not aware of the town's social order, such as I was at first, are guided into a seat appropriate to their status. If an older woman of a shaykhly family arrives late, women sitting in seats appropriate for the high-ranking woman will stand or shift to the side to make room in the appropriate area. Sometimes two or three persons must change position.

Mistakes are occasionally made and subtle challenges to seating orders sometimes occur. Once at a public Quranic reading, a young woman who was in a seat intended for persons of high status did not rise to make way for an elderly woman of high rank. No one said anything directly to her, but the person next to the young woman immediately rose and gave her seat to the newcomer, although she was herself of high status. There was a brief discussion about this act between the two women. Finally, enough space was found for both women to sit in the same area. Ten minutes later someone called the young woman away, perhaps intentionally. Her seat was immediately taken by the elderly shaykhly woman.

> November 23. In a manner appropriate for the mourning that was still going on, while we were talking quietly at Shaykh Ibrahim's, a guest arrived. She was the daughter of a client-tribe *bidār*, a day laborer who works in the orchards. Since she had been away visiting in Rustaq, this was her first visit to the shaykh's family after the death of his son. She circled the room twice,

once awkwardly squatting while walking, holding the hands of each family member and crying
loudly in a high-pitched tone. The second time
around, still squatting as she moved, she just
shook hands. She was unsure what to do with
me and finally shook hands with me once.

Rank at a large formal gathering is indicated by
how new arrivals are greeted. The main decision a
person must make is whether to stand up or remain
seated when greeting. To make this decision, one has
to know the nuances of local status and how recent
prior gatherings have ranked participants. Mastering
this etiquette with precision was always difficult for
me. Shaykhly women rise to greet one another; even
older women do so for younger ones. Shaykhly women
also stand for older women of slightly lesser status.
However, they remain seated to greet women of very
low status, no matter how old they are, such as those
of slave descent, or from client tribal groups, or from
the families of their retainers.

There is no formal introduction of persons, and
names are never directly asked. Women are expected
to know who is present; if they do not, they can only
ask discreetly after the gathering. Salutations are brief
but personal. Each woman says the name of a person
when she shakes her hand, if she knows it. No one
greets a group collectively. The person being greeted
replies, "You have come." The newcomer then sits
down and remains seated without changing her place
until she leaves. At departure, the same round of

Figure 9.   Men's guest room. Photograph by Birgitte Grue.

handshaking occurs, with the remaining persons re-plying, "You are leaving." Clasping one's left hand on top of the two clasped right hands by the person of lesser status indicates a high degree of inequality be-tween the handshakers.

Food served at formal gatherings varies in quality and quantity depending upon the wealth of the host household and the status of the guests; the order in which the food is served shows little variation. A poor household may serve canned rather than fresh fruit, but still it serves fruit. Except for extremely large gatherings, when two dishes may circulate separately, one large dish is first presented to the highest-rank-ing persons in the room. The dish is then circulated slowly around the room, together with a small bowl of water for rinsing fingers. After each sweet dish, un-sweetened coffee spiced with cardamom is offered. The small cup is filled and handed to the drinker as many times as it is not refused. The guest communi-cates that she has had enough by shaking the cup slightly from side to side when she returns it.

Good manners require that only one or two cups be accepted at a time and that the coffee be drunk quickly since it is served three or four times to all guests during the course of a visit, and only a few cups are circulating. Sometimes very sweet tea is also offered. It is not necessary for a guest to drink every time she is offered coffee. After a few cups, a guest can refuse subsequent ones by saying, "I do not want it." The filled cup is then offered to the woman sitting next to her.

Serving is often done by the youngest married woman of the household or, on formal occasions, by descendants of slaves. A young woman of shaykhly descent never serves persons of very low rank. She merely places the platter of food and the thermos of coffee in front of them, and they help themselves. After eating and drinking, persons of low status sometimes stand and serve members of the shaykhly family and other guests one more time.

If the occasion is a celebration, women paint their faces with saffron and mahaleb. Each woman is given a handful of the herbs diluted in a little water with which she paints her forehead, her temples, and sometimes her cheeks. Younger women sometimes use a pocket mirror to ensure the neat application of the paste. Occasionally a dab is placed next to the nostrils. The rich, yellow-orange color of the saffron and the dark red of the mahaleb are considered to be beautiful on the skin. Women say that the smell of these herbs is sexually stimulating. Women apply the leftover herbal pastes to the faces and ears of their children. Face painting is a highly valued activity, and some young shaykhly women paint their foreheads daily. It is often done at both formal and informal gatherings if the women involved can afford it. The colors flake off the skin within a few hours, and women are careful not to disturb the paint when washing themselves so that it remains on the skin as long as possible. Once Salma reprimanded me in a friendly way for washing it off too quickly.

Aromatics also play an important part in social life. Some aromatics are dry, ground herbs, a pinch of which is taken, sniffed, and then rubbed on one's clothes. Incense is burned on a charcoal brazier. Each woman comes up to the brazier in turn, lifts her tunic, and perfumes her pantaloons. Again, incense can be used at any gathering regardless of the level of formality, and women often fumigate their children's clothes with it. Finally, a tray of perfumes is brought out, signaling that the time for departure is near. Each woman takes a dab from the various bottles and hands it to her neighbor. These range from expensive French or Indian perfumes to men's Vaseline hair tonic, which is dabbed on the hands and face.[1]

Gatherings vary in size and formality, but all follow more or less the same format. Conversations remain on a general plane—who has recently given birth or had a miscarriage, what preparations are being made for the holidays, a new embroidery stitch for pantaloons. Older women and those of higher status tend to dominate the conversations. Other women usually remain silent until they are spoken to directly. The reason for the gathering is usually obvious to the participants and is in any case almost never explicitly mentioned.

Participation in formal visiting indicates that a woman has become an adult capable of representing her household in the community. As an adult, she is no longer confined solely to the more private world of members of the family cluster and close neighbors. Age, the mastery of appropriate etiquette, and a household's composition are the principal considerations that come into play in deciding when a woman may begin to participate in formal visiting. Young

Figure 10.   Woman in guest room. Photograph by Birgitte Grue.

brides usually refrain from taking part until a year or
two after marriage, by which time they often have
given birth to a first child, but if a woman remains
unmarried, she begins to participate in formal visiting
by her mid-twenties at the latest. Schooling often de-
lays participation in formal visiting patterns, especially among shaykhly families.

High status in Hamra does not guarantee greater
seclusion and confinement to the household, as is
the case, for example, in wealthy households in the
smaller towns of Morocco. The opposite is true of
Hamra. Shaykhly women who have the least household and outside labor to perform play prominent
roles in formal visiting networks. They have more visiting obligations than nonshaykhly women because of
their larger family clusters and their loftier status.

Two notable events that call for at least one formal
visit from female representatives of every household
in Hamra are births, for which there is a three-week
visiting period, called the murabbiya, and deaths, for
which there is a period of condolence ('aza'), which
ranges from a week to over four months, depending
on the age, sex, and status of the deceased. The number of times women visit during these occasions
depends on the status of the household, whether
the neighborly ties are maintained, and whether
the household is part of the same family cluster. A
shaykhly woman was mathematically precise with me
in explaining the number of visits required: one visit
for a household of slave descent, two visits for all
other nonshaykhly households, and daily if a house-

hold belongs to the same family cluster. Women of nonshaykhly descent visit once at births and deaths of the descendants of slaves, three or four times for close neighbors, and daily for members of the same family cluster.

Not all women in a household need show up for every birth or death; in fact, there is a tendency for older women to represent their households for condolences, and for younger women to visit after births. This division of labor may relate in part to cohort groups, since older women are more likely to know adults who have died and of course older women have more status than younger ones. If the death is of a person of high status, all women of a household visit, but not at the same time, because of the responsibilities of childcare.

As mentioned earlier, a neighbor never accompanies a woman if she is visiting her family, but she may be included in a visit to unrelated households. Nonshaykhly women usually prefer to visit households with which they are unfamiliar in groups of two or three, with either relatives or close neighbors. Shaykhly women often visit in large groups of seven or eight, their greater numbers making their arrival all the more formidable.

Formal visiting in the community occurs frequently. Over a period of two months Nasra went to eight murabbiyas, two condolences, and one marriage-contract celebration. Her own household held a large public reading of the Quran, to which men and women were separately invited.

As I have indicated earlier, for some of these formal occasions, there are separate, parallel visits for men. Certain agreements among men or even the visit of a person of high status may trigger formal coffee-drinking sessions among women who have nothing to do with the agreement and who do not meet or speak to the guest. The tribal leader once entertained a minister from Muscat. The visit occasioned an elaborate coffee-drinking session among the most important older shaykhly women of the oasis. They used the men's guest room of a shaykhly household adjacent to where the guest was being entertained. I was invited because by chance I happened to be walking with my daughter near the house. This particular occasion is analytically significant because it suggests that men and women are implicitly perceived as occupying parallel social positions. It also implies a recognition by men of the social importance of women's formal coffee-drinking sessions.

Visiting After Childbirth

Birth is a strictly private affair. Women conceal the fact of pregnancy until the last possible moment. Most women give birth at home, assisted by their mothers, a midwife, and close family members. Immediately after a birth, news spreads all over town. A period of intense visiting by women of the community lasts for the next twenty-five days. The new mother is served a tonic of fenugreek (*hulba*) and is fed a diet rich in meat for the next three weeks. She is made to lie down on a steel cot at the head of the room where women are received. Sitting or lying down, she greets all visitors. The child is swathed and placed, often in a small cardboard box, in a separate room. The infant's head is anointed with saffron or mahaleb, and his eyes are blackened with kohl. Very little attention is given to the infant in public, regardless of its sex. Unless I asked, the sex and name of infants were rarely mentioned to me, and there are no differences in women's visiting patterns whether the child is male or female, the firstborn or the tenth child. The child is often not seen, although occasionally the cardboard box with the infant in it is placed in the lap of a shaykhly woman of high status. She looks at the child with no comment, and the infant is then quickly returned to a separate room.

It is clear that the focal point of the murabbiya is not the child but the woman who has given birth. She is placed in a bed in a seat of honor and higher than everyone else. Surrounded by her closest family members, she may rest and let her family greet the guests as they come and go. She may actively take part in the conversation. Women visit her because she has given birth, not to see the child, and they expect to see her close family members next to her. If the child becomes sick and dies soon afterward—this happened several times during my stay in Hamra—the death does not prevent the visiting for the allotted three weeks. Implicitly, the child's death does not diminish the fact that the mother had given birth to a live child. This event is kept separate from condolences. There is no public mourning for the death of infants, because a child of only a few days or weeks is too young to have made any social impact in the community. A neighbor confided once to me that she and her husband cried when their first son died, but they did so only when they were alone. When infant deaths occur, mothers never shed tears publicly or show other signs of mourning. It is an act of God, which is not to be challenged. Visitors avoid mention of the child's death.

The usual pattern of coffee gatherings is followed for murabbiyas: the serving of fruits, dates, and coffee; the burning of incense; the offering of mahaleb or saffron and, finally, perfumes. Once the crowds of the first few days thin out, the atmosphere becomes less formal. So long as no visitor of high status is present, seating etiquette is relaxed. Once shaykhly and non-shaykhly women find themselves together, visits become more formal. Sometimes the tension is obvious.

> January 9. I accompanied my shaykhly neighbor Zayna, her mother-in-law, two of her sisters-in-law, and three other women, one of whom was the wife of a bidar, and hence of client status, to a murabbiya. We walked to an area next to the market where less wealthy people and descendants of slaves live. Our group was large, and we walked in file down narrow alleys to avoid the main road close to the market. On our arrival, our hosts exchanged greetings with us in a routine manner. The young mother lay back on

her couch and pretended to sleep during the entire visit. The shaykhly women talked among themselves. The women of the host household remained silent in the background. After a quick serving of tinned pineapples and mangoes, coffee and dates, mahaleb was offered, followed by incense and perfume. The infant, now fifteen days old, swaddled and with eyes heavily blackened with kohl, was brought in and placed in a bundle in the laps of some of the shaykhly women, but little attention was paid to her.

The bidar's wife stood up and handed various pots, pans, mirrors, and blankets that were on the shelves in the room to the shaykhly women so that they could examine them. I asked our hostess where she had bought these. "In Muscat," she replied. A price was quoted for one of the objects. There was no bargaining, although one of the shaykhly women remarked, "One can get a bigger tray for that price." One shaykhly woman took a blanket. Zayna took a few dishes. No money was exchanged.

On our way home, we walked along the last row of houses at the upper edge of the oasis, also an area where poor people and descendants of slaves live. The ground was littered with open tin cans and garbage where cats prowled. Many older women came out of their homes to greet us. There was handshaking with bowed heads and even hand kissing. We were offered many invitations to come and have coffee. Zayna gave a ryal, approximately three dollars, to an old woman. Another old woman, black, mumbled audibly behind our backs, "They don't want to come and visit us."

There is an economic side to the murabbiya that is not an essential feature but that is present in almost all households except those of shaykhly status. Hostesses place a few objects they wish to sell on their wall shelves. Visitors are always delighted to look at these objects and touch them although there is no obligation to buy. In general, nonshaykhly women buy very few items on these occasions. Sometimes only one or two objects are offered for sale; at other times there are entire shelves of objects. Prices are quoted on request, but no money is exchanged during the visit. Settlement is always later.

Visits to unrelated households rarely last more than thirty or forty minutes. The various stages of the visit all proceed at a brisk pace. Very often women attend two or even three murabbiyas in the same afternoon, or they might attend a murabbiya and then go to a condolence, in which case they do not paint their faces.

Consolation or Mourning

Unlike murabbiyas, which last as long and take the same form in shaykhly and nonshaykhly households, the period of mourning or consolation varies considerably in length, depending on the age, sex, and status of the deceased. As mentioned earlier, infants are not publicly mourned, because they have not yet become socially important. Young children who die at the age of four or five can be mourned publicly for a week, although in practice this may last no more than two or three days. A man formally mourns the loss of his wife for fifteen days; a widow past childbearing mourns her husband between fifteen days and a month, depending on his status. A younger widow mourns her husband for the full, Quranically sanctioned period of four months and ten days. This latter period is much longer because under Islamic law a woman cannot remarry for this period of time to ensure that she is not pregnant by her first husband at the time of remarriage. A widow in inner Oman does not go outside her household for the entire period of mourning, even to fetch a bucket of drinking water from the head of the falaj.

Both men and women acknowledge that private mourning may go on for much longer than the formal, public periods. This is especially true in the case of the death of children. Women spoke with me privately with great sadness about their children who died in infancy. If I asked a woman how many children she had, she invariably included the deceased ones as well and specified their sex. A husband and mother may also be mourned privately for long periods, years in some cases. Such private mourning becomes apparent because a woman does not perfume herself, dye her hands with henna, or paint her face with saffron or mahaleb.

Just as for the murabiyya, the number of days a woman attends an 'aza' depends on her relation with the deceased's household. Family members come every day. At least one woman from each household in Hamra comes once during the mourning period. For the longer mourning periods for widows, two or three visits are considered appropriate.

Shortly after our arrival in Hamra, the oldest son of Shaykh Ibrahim died unexpectedly. I attended the mourning for this individual of high status almost daily.

> November 5. Around noon, my husband told me of the death of Ahmad, Shaykh Ibrahim's son, and told me he saw women walking in the direction of Shaykh Ibrahim's house. I fed Amal her lunch, then went with her to the shaykh's house. As I approached the house, I could hear a low, sing-song hum that never became loud but filled the entrance and the entire courtyard. The men's guest room was filled with people, and some men pointed me to a room on the first floor of the house where many women were sitting, for once in no discernible order, sobbing quietly. This was the only occasion in Hamra when I did not see a clear order in the seating. Indeed, some women were standing in the middle of the room, and the descendants of slaves mixed freely with the others.
>
> Some women embraced one another as they cried. Others hid their faces behind their veils. Some softly chanted, "My father [*abuyi*, i.e., my

God], Ahmad has left, my father," and their bodies swayed back and forth. The room was dark, but after a while I noticed that some of the sisters of the deceased were lying on mattresses on the ground with blankets wrapped around them, in spite of the heat, as if they were dead or asleep. 'Azza, the widow, sat half-wrapped in a blanket, beating her fists against her chest, rocking back and forth, and crying. She was attended by several older women who also offered water to members of the immediate family. The whole scene was extraordinarily moving, and my eyes filled with tears.

In the afternoon, around 4 P.M., I returned to Shaykh Ibrahim's house. By now, the mourning was much more formal. Everyone had moved to the large guest room upstairs. 'Azza and some of her husband's sisters were on mattresses at one far side of the room. The descendants of slaves were at the opposite side of the room. Tribal women had begun to arrive by pickup trucks from the entire area. They sat all around the room. The descendants of slaves were roasting coffee beans, but I did not stay long enough to drink any. The immediate relatives of the deceased took shifts in mourning out loud. Asila began, then someone else took over. Most of the women present were older, and I noticed very few children present. Before leaving, I shook hands all around. 'Azza made a point of extending her hand to shake mine.

November 6. I went briefly to the mourning this afternoon. Some older shaykhly women, the mother of Shaykh Ahmad, 'Azza, and some of Ahmad's sisters sat in the guest room receiving guests who came from the entire region. Few women were talking; the atmosphere was very formal. Coffee, dates, and fruits were served by descendants of slaves, who also cooked meals for persons who had traveled from afar. Some of the family members appeared exhausted. Indeed, they took turns to lie down and rest. In a side room, other family members of Shaykh Ibrahim were sitting apart. I accepted their invitation to sit with them. Before leaving, I asked where Shaykh Ahmad's mother was. I was then ushered back into the main room, where she lay on a mattress at one end of the room. I had not recognized her before, because she was unable to speak. I shook hands with her and left.

November 7. The atmosphere at the 'aza' is much more relaxed than yesterday, and there are fewer people. Some women laughed because Amal trailed behind me, seriously shaking hands with everyone present in good Omani style. Again I was invited into a side room where most of the younger shaykhly family members were sitting, including some women with young children. The handful of children present were playing with balloons and eating cookies. This room was a sort of makeshift nursery to keep the younger children busy and to prevent them from disturbing people in the main mourning area. Shaykh Ahmad's mother in the main guest room was holding a child in her lap. 'Azza, dressed in black from head to foot, was breastfeeding her youngest daughter. Life was going on.

Intensive visiting by women from Hamra and surrounding towns and villages continued for over a week and then diminished. All households of the shaykhly family cluster had someone visit daily for about a month and then at intervals spaced further apart until the end of the mourning period. 'Azza's mother, her two sisters, her father's second wife, or stepmother, her half-sister, her half-brother's wife, and the sisters of her husband who no longer lived in their father's household visited daily during the entire period. One sister, herself a widow, moved back into her father's house for the mourning period. One sub-cluster of close kin that became evident during the mourning was Azza's half-sister, her stepmother, and her half-brother's wife, all of whom visited daily but for a short period, usually toward the end of the day. After a month, two of the deceased's sisters who were attending intermediate school in Hamra ceased attending the 'aza' in the afternoon so that they could study.

After the first few weeks, as the uninterrupted flow of visitors diminished to a trickle, the 'aza' became much more sedate. The widow was usually accompanied by one or two of her four children. She and some of her sisters-in-law began to embroider caps for their sons or husbands. Occasionally someone picked up a Quran and chanted a chapter. Conversation was subdued, but there was some laughter and a great deal of playing with children. Sometimes a woman arrived who for some reason or another had not visited before. Then faces would be hidden behind veils as the visitor went around the room shaking hands. Soon the women present began to sob again.

Four months and ten days is a long time to be confined to a household, even a large one, to be idle, and to be prepared to receive guests at any time. Toward the end of the mourning period, the widow confided to me that she was finding her immobility difficult. Once the official period of mourning was over, one of the first things she did was to resume doing some of the housework. One afternoon just after the mourning, I found her happily making bread. Close family members also find the long period of mourning to be difficult because in principle they cannot show themselves to be cheerful, wear beautiful clothes or makeup, or paint mahaleb or saffron on their forehead. About a month before the end of the mourning, I encountered one of 'Azza's sisters at a murabiyya, where she was rubbing saffron on her forehead and looking at herself in a small pocket mirror. She rubbed it off immediately afterward.

On the evening of the last day of mourning, the widow formally washes her hair and discards her black clothes. She wears white garments for about a

week, during which time there is a final wave of visitors from all the neighboring towns and villages, as
well as from Hamra. Again there is a great deal of
"formal" crying. Persons of slave origin no longer
cook and serve guests, and all housework is resumed
by the women of the household.

An 'aza' of the size of that for Shaykh Ahmad
contrasts sharply with those for persons of more modest status. A man of lower status is mourned by a
handful of persons. After the initial couple of days of
intensive visiting from people of the community, the
'aza' becomes little more than a waiting period until
normal daily routines can be resumed.

> February 21. Jukha told me with a sad face that
> her sister's husband had died yesterday. I visited
> the family of the deceased on my own. His fam-
> ily lived high up on the hill, close to an area
> where many descendants of slaves lived. The
> widow was in the main room, dressed in black,
> together with some fifteen women. There was
> no crying out loud. Visitors just shook hands
> and maintained a serious look. I sat down and
> talked generalities with my neighbors. The at-
> mosphere was such that at times one almost
> forgot it was a mourning. Mournings are also
> expensive. Oranges, bananas, coffee, and tea
> were served every half-hour. Ibtisama, a descen-
> dant of a slave who lived next door, served the
> guests. Her four children hung around the door.
> She constantly had to tell them to play farther

away. The house was too small to accommodate
men as well as women; so the men sat outside
on a mat in the shade of a nearby guesthouse.

The humble status of the deceased is obvious
from accumulated details—the small number of kin
present, the location of the house, even the lack of
restraint on the part of the children present. Nonetheless, no matter how modest the household, a descendant of a slave is called in to serve guests, at least for
the initial few days of the mourning period. This action distinguishes the households of "the freeborn"
(*al-aḥrār*) from those of slave origin and client tribal
groups.

Quran Recitals

A public recital of the Quran takes place when an
individual or household wishes to thank God for
good fortune or to ensure continued good fortune.
One may occur if someone escapes uninjured from an
automobile accident, if one recovers from a serious
illness, if a woman wishes to be pregnant or is pregnant and wishes all to go well, or if a household has
several healthy children and wishes them to continue
to grow up strong.

A woman who organizes a khatma—men orga-
nize them, too—calls on the wife of the tribal leader or
some other leading shaykhly woman to set up a date.
Quranic recitals usually occur in the morning. The

news then spreads by word of mouth among shaykhly women and neighbors. Most of the shaykhly women who know how to read and who do not have conflicting obligations attend. Older women nearly always do so, as well as younger ones who can arrange to leave their children with someone. The one full-time female Quranic teacher is always invited. Literacy is not necessary in order to attend, but it is of course very prestigeful to be able to participate by reading a chapter.

As each woman enters the room where the Quranic recital will be held, she takes a printed section of the Quran from a box kept in a prominent place for the occasion, which contains the entire Quran but in separately bound sections. After a brief greeting to those present, each woman sits in a place appropriate to her rank and begins to read out loud. Soon the entire room rings out with women reading the Quran individually, each separately and without any attempt to read in unison. When a woman finishes a chapter, she may begin another or wait until all the recitals are completed, usually after an hour. Afterward, coffee, fruit, and other sweet dishes are served. Incense is sometimes burned throughout the entire reading. Once the perfumes are offered, everyone goes home.

Seating arrangements are very important at Quranic recitals because these are formal gatherings that are attended by persons of the highest status in the community, the wives, sisters, and daughters of prominent shaykhs. The household organizing the Quranic recital makes sure that everyone is seated appropriately. If there are several roomfuls of people,

then there are clusters of high-ranking, literate individuals, capable of reciting the Quran, in each room.
If the two wives of one shaykh attend, they are di-
rected to separate rooms, each with their respective
daughters and daughters-in-law. Most Quranic recitals involve women only, but some elaborate ones
have men reading the Quran and involve the sacrifice
of an animal for a feast. On these occasions women
busy themselves cooking and distributing food to as
large a number of people as possible in a lavish display of hospitality.

The purpose of a Quranic recital on one level is to
have the entire Quran read in one's home because this
reading in itself is seen as a way of continuing one's
good fortune. A Quranic recital is only possible, however, by calling upon shaykhly women because to date
they continue to be the best educated women of the
community. There needs to be a fairly large number of
persons reading simultaneously in order to finish the
entire Quran within an hour. The very presence of
these women and the fact that they are divided into
known subclusters that rival one another for power
and prestige make seating arrangements especially
important, and women know this. Households are
not obliged to offer Quranic recitals, but doing so is a
means of enhancing household prestige.

Formal Visiting: Analytical Implications

Simmel (1950: 12) characterizes a "party" or large
gathering as possessing (1) a specific external setup

(i.e., food, dress, and specific forms of behavior), (2) the curtailing of individuality, (3) the intensification of external and sensuous attraction to make up for this curtailment, and (4) the formation of subgroups. The formal gatherings of women in Hamra fit Simmel's characterization: an emphasis on food and, except for mournings, scents, the curtailed expression of personal feelings, the avoidance of private or personal topics of discussion, and the formation of subgroups of conversing women. These subgroups tend to consist of women of more or less equal social rank, since seating is by order of status and sheer distance prevents persons of highly divergent ranks from readily speaking with one another. Throughout these gatherings, women remain in one place and do not change groups quickly, as would be the case in Western-style parties where etiquette pressures people to move among clusters of individuals. The departure of some women and the arrival of others produce some circulation of individuals, but because the principle of seating by order of status is preserved, this circulation is far from random. Persons of lower status never, even if a guest room is nearly empty, sit in places understood to be set aside for persons of much higher status.

It is not too far-fetched to see a resemblance between these gatherings and Simmel's description (1950: 114) of a "modern" ball, which he describes as a sublimated form of a large party, in which there is a "momentary peculiar intimacy of couple" (in the case of Hamra, a temporary juxtaposition of women of dif-

ferent family or neighbor clusters) and a "constant
change among couples" (visitors in the case of
Hamra). Simmel adds:

. . . the physical nearness between total strangers is made
possible by two factors. On the one hand, all participants
in the ball are guests of a host who, however loose their
relations may be to him, nevertheless guarantees a certain
reciprocal security and legitimation. On the other hand,
relations are impersonal and as it were anonymous, because of the magnitude of the group and the associated
formalism of behavior.

Obviously, most guests are not "total strangers"
in the case of Hamra, except on occasions such as the
mourning for Shaykh Ahmad, for which many visitors were unknown to many of the guests and came
from the capital and outside the region. Nonetheless,
mutually known status distinctions in Hamra and the
tightly knit and exclusive nature of family clusters and
even some small groups of close neighbors create sufficient social distance among the populace for the formal analogy to hold. Except for brief meetings when
passing one another in the streets or at the falaj, many
women see one another only on these formal visits.

The atmosphere of these social gatherings becomes relaxed or formal depending on the status,
number, and relationships of the women present.
When the circle of women present is small and fairly
equal in status, halfway between a small group and a
"party" (in Simmel's sense), the gathering can be relaxed and almost intimate. When persons of disparate
status are present together and numbers increase, the

"party" becomes highly stylized. These cases are the two polar extremes of what actually takes place. A range of intermediate situations occur that depend not only on the status of the persons involved but to some extent on their personalities or chance topics of common interest. My daughter and the idea of adoption, unknown in a formal sense in Oman, were such topics.

Employment opportunities away from Hamra have had a direct impact on women's visiting networks because it has made many households less dependent economically on shaykhly patrons and has provided alternatives to local patron-client ties. Some nonshaykhly men have been very successful in their work away from the oasis. The men and women of these households have partially withdrawn from formal visiting because of the disparity between the higher status they have achieved elsewhere and the lower status they are expected to display with the shaykhs of the oasis. Other households continue to behave as clients when they visit shaykhs, but they make such visits less frequently than they did in the past, when such visits were often daily. Nonetheless, no household in Hamra has as yet ceased completely to take part in formal visiting. Each social gathering represents a practical manifestation of social ranking in Hamra. To cease visiting, for both shaykhly and nonshaykhly persons, is to withdraw from the community. Giving and receiving visits is an essential part of acquiring and maintaining status in the oasis. These relations are far from fixed, and there are recent dramatic shifts of status for some persons. Thus, one person of slave origin who has risen to high rank in the army sits with the shaykhs when he returns to the oasis for the most important Muslim holidays. Nevertheless, the system of social ranking has not yet undergone drastic redefinition.

NOTES

1.   For a detailed study of the various aromatics used in the United Arab Emirates, see Kanafani (1983). The use of spices, perfumes, dyes, jewelry and embroidered clothes is intended to beautify the food and body and to foster positive communication.

7.

CHILDREN

"All women want to marry. Why? Because they want children."
—Hamra, aged twenty, a mother of two children.

Motherhood

MOTHERHOOD is by far a woman's most honored role in inner Oman. It is only during the visiting period occurring after childbirth that a woman obtains her first social recognition among the women of the community. Having many children, especially sons, increases a woman's status considerably by making her later in life the female head of a large family cluster.[1] Having mature brothers or sons significantly facilitates a woman's chances for achieving prominence in the oasis community. Just as a woman retains close ties with her parents, especially her mother, there are very strong bonds between her and her children, which last throughout her life. As a woman becomes old herself, she is aware of the likelihood of spending her last days in the household of one of her children.

A woman pays dearly in health for the social prestige of having many children. Many women become physically exhausted from so many childbirths and frequent and dangerous complications that arise from pregnancy, including miscarriages. Infant mortality rates in Oman have stayed high until recently. A UNICEF report (1973: 41) estimated that in 1972 in Nizwa, the largest oasis in the Omani interior, 17.6 percent of children died in their first year, and 23.4 percent of children died before the age of two. These figures are tentative because of a tendency to under-report infant deaths. Nonetheless, they are in line with estimates in Egypt for the 1940s, where approximately 23 percent of village children died in their first year, with another 25 percent dying between the ages of one and four (Ammar, 1954: 112). Infant mortality is decreasing in Oman because of the opening of hospitals and clinics throughout the country. Oman's population is expected to double by the year 2000 (Birks and Sinclair, 1977b: 71). Nonetheless, women still acutely sense the precariousness of their children's lives in their first years.

In spite of the health hazards attendant on giving birth so frequently, women continue to desire many children, not only for the status, prestige, and future security associated with strong, healthy children, but because children are valued in themselves. The mother-child relationship is the most open and relaxed one that a woman can maintain. In a society where the direct expression of one's feelings is frowned upon, except in private among close family members, love for one's children can be publicly ackowledged. I often heard women say, "I love her (or him) very much," as they fed a child a choice morsel of food or dressed the child. When only relatives or close neighbors are present, women spontaneously caress their children. Both Nasra and Salma occasionally sat a little aside from other women and showered their infants with kisses on such occasions. Shaykhly women also show open affection for their children, both girls and boys.

One of the first questions I was always asked on meeting a new group of women was how many children I had. In almost every case, their reaction was identical: "Just one? You poor thing. Are you pregnant? No? Don't you want at least five?" When I have asked women how many children they wanted, some just laughed and treated my question as a joke. Others answered with numbers that ranged from four to ten. Still others, often older maried women with several children of their own, were startled by my question and then seriously answered, "As many as I can." Some women have heard of modern birth control techniques, such as the Pill, but none used family planning methods and few wished to do so. Some women told me that children were "tiring," but I met no one who said she wanted fewer than four. Birth control is perceived as something a woman may consider only if she has several children and if having another child would endanger her life.

To my question, "How many children do you have?" women of Hamra answered by telling me the number of times they gave birth to a live child, regardless of whether the child was still alive or not. They also disclosed the sex of their children. In some cases, I had to rephrase my questions to find out that only one out of four was still alive or three out of ten; in other cases, women volunteered which of their children were then still alive. This way of answering at first surprised me because it was so different from that of women in rural Morocco, who often answered similar questions from me by listing the names of their living children on their fingers, counting as they went along, as if they had never counted them before. In Oman the number of times a woman has given birth and the sex of each child are the important things that are remembered. Names of living children are never given unless they are specifically requested.

Adoption as it is known in the West—the legal granting of rights, including inheritance, to a child who is not biologically one's own—is not acknowledged in Islamic law and is unknown in Oman. Raising a child who belongs to neither parent is done only in cases of necessity, such as when both the child's parents die. Even then, it is usually done only by other relatives. My husband has recorded instances from intertribal raiding in the 1940s in the Dhahira region, near the border with the present-day United Arab Emirates, where tribal shaykhs have raised the children of assassinated allies. Such occurrences were extremely rare. If the child has no family cluster, he or she becomes the ward of the government and, under current arrangements, is raised by hospital staff. Some women told me of a child living at the Nizwa hospital in this way. When women heard that my child was adopted—a concept that I tried carefully to explain—they pitied me for not having given birth. Many never came to accept the idea that I regarded Amal as truly my daughter. One woman from a neighboring hamlet in the mountains, who had two small children of her own, exclaimed in amazement, "How can you raise a child that is not your own? I would not want to raise one of those." She pointed to a nearby group of children, who happened to be from her family cluster. My neighbor Rashida, who was childless, nonetheless envied me and said she would gladly have an adopted daughter, but she realized it was impossible for her to do so. As in other matters, Omani attitudes toward raising children who are not biologically one's own differ greatly from attitudes in North Africa, where women regularly raise children from infancy, whether they are relatives under Islamic law or aren't, and where these children are often well integrated in the family group.

> February. 20 At Shaykh Ibrahim's I mentioned that I had received a letter from my mother. I was asked to translate it. The letter concerned my younger sister, who had just given birth to a son. Afterward Sharifa said to me softly, "Your mother must love you very much. She must love you more than your sister." "Why do you say

that?" I asked. "Because you have no children. Mothers love their daughters who have no children more."

This conversation sticks in my mind, not only because it indicates how deeply rooted was the notion that an "adopted" child can never completely become one's own in Oman, but because it also points to the importance women attach to having at least one daughter. By implying that I must be very close to my mother, Sharifa was also paying me a compliment. Mothers and daughters see each other constantly in Hamra. A mother is usually a woman's most intimate confidante and the one person whom she can trust completely. Daughters help with housework and childcare. They are assured companions once a woman grows old. "I will massage your front and your back, and I promise you a handsome girl," an older woman who specialized in massaging infertile women once suggested to me. Sons are fine, but women without daughters are regarded as unfortunate.

Growing Up

Until it is three or four months old, an infant is expected only to drink and sleep. The child is bound in cloth most of the time to prevent movement of his arms and legs and spends large portions of time in a wooden cradle, sometimes a rocking one, hanging from the ceiling by a rope. The cradle is completely covered with a cloth to protect the child from flies and mosquitoes. A small Quran is usually kept at the head of the crib as protection (ḥifāẓ) against harm; charms are obtained from one of the female Quranic school-teachers. The cradle is hung in a side room (if there is one), away from visitors. The mother or grandmother comes to wash, change, feed and cuddle the child there. Sometimes makeshift disposable diapers are used, such as little strips of cloth that are placed under the child and then thrown away. If possible, women breastfeed, but many now supplement breastfeeding with bottles of milk that they place in the crib with the child. The breastfed child in Oman has a great advantage over the bottle-fed one because of the more frequent body handling. Bottle-fed babies are subject to diseases arising from the use of unboiled water and unsterilized bottles in a hot climate. However, if a woman discovers that she is pregnant again, she stops breastfeeding, because combining the two activities is considered to be harmful to the unborn child. If several children are born in close succession, some women find that they can no longer provide their own milk.

Forty days after birth, there is a ceremony called the "changing of clothes and bedding," during which the child is formally washed in the presence of women from the family cluster. If the child is a boy, money is placed on his chest, his hands and feet are hennaed, and women "make a great deal of noise" so that he will grow up strong. For a girl, the ceremony is less elaborate. Women do not "make noise," and no money is placed on her chest by relatives, but her hands and feet are hennaed. A shaykhly woman told me of this ceremony, which I didn't see during my stay. When I asked nonshaykhly women about the "noisemaking" at the ceremony, they said it was done only in shaykhly households, not in their own.

Women are very concerned about infants who cry a great deal. They attribute constant crying to colic and stomach ailments, which indeed occur regularly. The most common remedy for stomach ailments when I was in Hamra was a grippe syrup made in India; it was one of the few remedies available in the local market. The list of ingredients, listed both in English and Arabic on the bottle, included various fragrant oils such as anise, bicarbonate of soda, chloroform, and alcohol. This syrup was indeed effective in putting children to sleep.

When children are four or five months old, they begin to be seen much more on the laps of their mother or grandmother during the neighbors' visits. Mothers also begin to take their child on visiting rounds, especially to households within the family cluster. From now until the time the child learns to walk, he receives a great deal of attention, handling, and caressing from his mother. This is also the period when an older relative or a close neighbor often comes to hold and distract the child while the mother works at some of her household chores, either in the house or at the falaj. The child is not allowed to crawl very far. In general, walking rather than crawling is encouraged from the outset. Older shaykhly women tend not to take care of their grandchildren, and except for occasional cuddling, do not like young children to be around them and to interrupt their conversation.

In households where there are several young women with children, each woman is responsible for her own child. If she hears a child other than her own crying, she does not go to comfort him but says to the mother, "Your child is crying." Once, on an informal visit to a shaykhly household, I picked up a screaming infant girl that had been left alone in a side room. The infant immediately stopped crying in my arms, and I waited for her mother to return, which she did a few minutes later. The mother, whom I knew well, was not annoyed by my action, but the young adolescent who was accompanying her quickly repressed a slightly mocking peel of laughter.

The great amount of attention that mothers give their youngest child often creates emotional trauma for the children just a year or two older. I have seen some children aged two or three throw violent temper tantrums or go through long periods of whining when their mother paid little attention to them while she tended to the younger child or did her housework. In such cases, some other household member, often the grandmother, takes over and cares for the older child until he reaches an age when he can fend for himself, usually around the age of four or five. Then the peer group absorbs him. From birth until the age of three or four, both boys and girls frequently cling to the mother or mother's surrogate (such as a grand-mother), hiding under their veils, especially in un-familiar situations. Younger children often took weeks to relax in my presence.

Once children learn to walk and talk, men take a more visible interest in them. Nasra's father often took his two-year-old granddaughter for car rides in the afternoon. The girl's father also played with her frequently at home. On Thursday afternoons, Salma's husband took his two older sons of three and five to wash in the men's bathing area next to a nearby mosque.

In Oman it is the girls who wear pants. A girl's legs are covered from the time she is born. From birth onward, girls are dressed in brightly colored tunics while boys wear tunics of solid colors, often in pastel shades. In the past, children of both sexes wore jew-elry when young, but this custom is changing. Most children, especially boys, no longer do so except in rural areas. In the cool winter months, young children of both sexes wear head caps decorated with machine-embroidered geometric designs. In recent years, im-ported baby clothes, mostly knits, have become avail-able in the market, but girls continue to wear long pants, and children of both sexes, regardless of the weather, wear long-sleeved clothing so that almost the entire body is covered.

Young children are called "unknowing" (*jāhil*) and sometimes even "crazy" (*majnūn*), and they are not held responsible for their words or actions. If a child does something socially unacceptable, such as removing all his clothes, he is admonished and forced immediately to put his clothes on again. "What you have done is shameful ['ayb]," a mother scolds. But more often, if, for example, a child breaks something or grabs morsels of food from the common plate when women drink coffee together, he is not scolded. It is the mother who is reprimanded by her peers if she shows too much disapproval of her child's bad behavior. "Let him eat," a woman might say. "The poor child. He does not know." Social knowledge is expected of a child by the age of five or six, but even then scolding or corporal punishment is rare. A child is never pushed around or lied to; he is allowed his own will so long as he hurts no one. If the child is too boisterous or throws a temper tantrum that disturbs adult activities, someone takes him into a separate room. Adults seldom lose their temper.

> November 3. Around 11 A.M., Muza came to my house and accompanied Amal and me to Shaykh 'Abdalla's, to which we had been invited for the holiday meal. She told me she was first going to Suhayr's (an Egyptian who was our neighbor for several weeks) to invite her as well. Muza showed obvious signs of trepidation as she knocked at the door and whispered to me, "Miryam, I am afraid." I reassured her. Neither Suhayr nor her husband, who taught at the local intermediate school, was expecting the invitation. We had to wait in the guest area while Suhayr dressed and fed her three-year-old son a

bottle of milk, which I thought strange since we were invited for a meal. Muza was extremely uncomfortable and squirmed a great deal when she was seated. This was due in part to Suhayr's husband, who remained with us to serve us oranges. Muza was not used to sitting with an unrelated man.

At the shaykh's, the atmosphere was extremely formal. Susan, an American Peace Corps volunteer who lived with her husband in a house more than a kilometer outside Hamra, sat beside one of the shaykh's wives. I sat next to the other. Suhayr was placed next to the wife of the shaykh's eldest son. The shaykh's four married daughters and his two daughters-in-law were also present.

Having already eaten separately with her husband, Susan left after coffee and fruit. Suhayr and I were then ushered into Shaykha's bedroom, where we were offered a meal of skewered meat, roast meat, rice, and a green sauce made with lemon. Suhayr did not touch the rice and had constantly to be urged to eat the other dishes. After the meal we returned to the guest room, where tea was served, probably in Suhayr's honor because Egyptians were known to prefer it, but she refused to drink it. [Out of earshot of Omanis, many Egyptians expressed constant concern for the cleanliness of food in Omani houses.] Suhayr's son, excited by the large number of children present, took some straw fans and began hitting other children with them. There was laughter from some older Omani children and tears from the younger ones and my Amal. Suhayr scolded her son, but he did not stop. Then she lost her temper, slapped him, picked up a nearby stick from the floor, and threatened him with it. The atmosphere in the room became glacial and everyone stared in silence. Some shaykhly women turned their heads to the side, frowning slightly and averting their eyes. The silence continued for a few minutes. Fortunately, Suhayr's husband came to fetch her a few minutes later, and everyone left.

To Omani women, Suhayr's loss of temper in public at a formal gathering and her reaching the point of hitting her son indicated a scandalous lack of self-control. The fact that Suhayr's son was only three and too young to be held responsible for his actions made his mother's conduct all the more shocking. The incident also reflects how cool social relations can be between Omanis and Egyptians who come to work in Oman and how mutually incomprehending they can be of one another.

As a child matures, the peer group exerts an ever-increased influence, the separation of the sexes becomes more pronounced, and formal education at the Quranic schools and at government schools becomes more important. From the age of five, all children are expected to stay clear of adults on formal occasions, including those times when women receive visitors.

This is true even if the guests are from the family cluster, except of course for special occasions and feast days when children either sit quietly in groups a little apart from adults, listening and watching intently the actions of their elders, or in a side room, where they whisper so as not to make too much noise. Mothers constantly admonish older children who remain around them, "Go and play."

Since family cluster members tend to live side by side, a child's playmates are often those related to him, and a friendship begun in childhood likely continues through a lifetime. Children of different social status play together. The children attend the same government primary school, and the boys play on the same soccer team, and thus this mixing is encouraged. Status barriers, however, still exist, especially between the children of shaykhly families and others. My husband notes, for example, that only children of slave descent sing or dance at the school pageants organized by Egyptian schoolteachers. The sons of shaykhs read the Quran. Among young girls, the jokes and sharp comments at informal gatherings can often be cruel when different status groups are mixed.

At the age of five, boys and girls are expected to begin forming separate play groups, although sexual segregation is not yet strictly enforced. Girls play in the immediate vicinity of their own houses and those of close family members and neighbors. They also walk along the paths to the falaj. Boys, on the other hand, usually play farther away from the house. Many go to the ball fields and other open spaces sur-

Figure 11. "By the time they reach eight or nine years of age, girls begin to assist in household chores." Photograph by Birgitte Grue.

rounding the oasis. Few boys and no girls go to the
market, which is open only in the morning when
school-age children are in school. If boys show too
much interest in what women are doing or talking
about, and my presence occasionally awakened their
curiosity, they are shooed away.

By the time they reach eight or nine year of age,
girls begin to assist in household chores. They carry
water on their heads, sweep floors, wash clothes, and
take care of younger children. By the age of ten, they
begin wearing a head shawl, although they often allow it to slip off. Boys may replace their fathers if the
family has a shop in the market. If no one else is
available, they may also care for their younger brothers and sisters. After sunset, children of both sexes in
the same household are together again. In wealthier
households that had televisions and (pre-1982) the
generators to run them, youngsters clustered around
the television set to watch Egyptian soap operas.

Achieving Adulthood

Childhood is in essence the period when an individual begins to master the nuances of proper adult
comportment and judgment: how to conduct oneself
in public, when to visit, how to talk. The adult is
expected not only to know these conventions but to
have sufficient self-control to abide by them. Adults
are held responsible for the consequences if they
do not.

Children routinely make social blunders, but they are rarely scolded in public. They are expected to recognize their own mistakes as they mature. For a week or two, a ten-year-old girl who lived up the falaj from us began following me when I went out visiting and also calling at my house. She perceived me as a school-teacher, as did many people since schoolteachers were the only female foreigners in the oasis at that time. She pleaded with me to visit her house and invited me at unusual times when visitors are not expected. One day she called at my house at noon, took me by the hand, and insisted that I come to her house for coffee. She was not satisfied when I promised that I would go after the afternoon prayer, a more appropriate time for visiting. She continued to pull me by the hand. Unused to such insistence, I finally went with her and took Amal along. The girl's mother showed no evident surprise at our arrival and seemed to be expecting us. She offered us rice and fish in a separate room and coffee and dates on a mat outside the house. She did not admonish her daughter that this was not a time for visiting neighbors (I later learned that our visit took the mother entirely by surprise), and she was hospitable to me.

This reluctance to point out mistakes even to one's own children, so long as no one is hurt or upset, certainly has no equivalent in Egypt or Morocco, two Arab countries in which I have lived for long periods of time. I never heard a woman in inner Oman say, "This is not right; try it this way," or, "You might hurt yourself if you do this"—familiar admonitions to any woman who has sat with her children in an American playground. The child is left alone to experiment. The mother will intervene only when she thinks the child might injure himself or break something. The same attitude of noninterference in the affairs of others is carried through into adulthood.

Although a child is seldom scolded for misconduct, he is rewarded for proper behavior. When I returned to Hamra in the fall of 1980 after an absence of several months, Salma's five-year-old son greeted me with a large smile. He then rushed to the family's orchard, where he picked handfuls of limes, some ripe and others not so ripe, which he poured into my lap. His mother and grandmother watched him, laughing a little at his boyish enthusiasm and also extremely proud of his show of hospitality.

Formal schooling, with its associated notion of clearly delineated grades, and the idea of calendar age are still recent phenomena. Childhood is not a clearly demarcated interval, and the concept of adolescence, a period of experimentation when a person is no longer a child but not yet fully adult, is unknown, at least in the Omani interior.

For girls, visiting in the community is the sign that one has achieved full adult status. The timing of the shift from child to adult depends not only on physical and social maturity but also on when a household is in need of another adult to assume certain responsibilities. The shift generally takes place after a woman has given birth to her first child.[2] Childless women and persons who remain unmarried also assume adult visiting responsibilities, generally at a later age than married persons. As a consequence, girls of equal age and social maturity find themselves assuming significantly different roles in the community. Thariyya was fifteen, unmarried, a student at the local girls' school, and not treated as an adult for most formal social occasions. Muza, also fifteen, was married and a student. Without children of her own, she continued to sit apart with other schoolgirls on formal occasions. Raqiya, sixteen, was married and had a one-year-old daughter. She participated fully in the formal visiting network. All these women are from shaykhly families, but individual circumstances allow some to be considered as adults while others are not. Hansen (1968: 114) describes the difficult situation of the "adolescent" girl and her social isolation in Bahrain. It is basically a time of waiting for marriage and children, the marks of adult status.

Education

Until 1971, Quranic schools were the only educational institutions available in Hamra (see Eickelman, 1980b). Quranic schools are still the only ones available in some remote villages, but in Hamra they have become preschools, which children attend until the age of six, when they enter the first grade of the government schools. Because of the crowding in these schools, there are two separate sessions, morning and afternoon.

In 1979 there were two Quranic schools for boys. Each was located next to a mosque and financed jointly by local resources and a small grant from the Ministry of Pious Endowments. Girls were taught by a woman teacher in her own house. She received a small monthly salary from the Ministry of Pious Endowments and a small monthly fee paid by the parents of the students. A second woman, of shaykhly status, also took students, mostly the daughters of shaykhs. Because girls have to pay tuition to learn how to recite the Quran, it is mostly the daughters of shaykhly and well-to-do families that master its proper recitation.

For households of higher status in Hamra, Quranic schools in the past have been fairly effective in teaching proper Quranic recitation. Children learned to master writing skills primarily in their home environment, not in Quranic schools. In Morocco, literacy among women was directly related to the availability of government schools, and almost all women over a certain age, regardless of their status, were illiterate, but I would estimate that in Hamra in 1980, some 50 percent of adult women of shaykhly status were literate and that this rate of literacy remained fairly constant across the generations. A few nonshaykhly women could also read the Quran. By *literacy*, I do not necessarily mean that persons could fully understand what they read, especially in the case of the Quran and other religious texts. Learning the proper recitation of the Quran does not necessarily imply an ability to understand its contents, since the language of the Quran differs substantially from contemporary Omani spoken Arabic and modern standard Arabic. Nor does an ability to recite the Quran necessarily imply the ability to write. Full literacy among the younger shaykhly generation was of course much more common. Young shaykhly women could and did read textbooks and occasional magazines in addition to the Quran. Many young girls of nonshaykhly status also attended school but were, as I shall explain, much more likely to drop out after a few years than their shaykhly counterparts.

Women consider the ability to read the Quran of great value. The Quran is not only recited publicly. Shaykhly women also chant it privately together with other religious books, either alone or with a small group of listeners. For most women, learning Quranic recitation is still the main motivation for becoming literate. The incentive to learn to read is strong among shaykhly women, old and young, since they can then actively participate in public readings of the Quran with other women of high status. I know one shaykhly woman, about fifty years old, who learned to read the Quran only five years before I was introduced to her.

The first government primary school in Hamra opened with two Jordanian teachers in 1971. It was for males only. In 1975 the first primary school classes were made available for females, and by 1979 the first two years of intermediate school were also taught in Hamra. Now the full three-year intermediate cycle is locally available, and the first two years of secondary school. At first these government schools admitted students regardless of age. Today only children of the appropriate age may attend regular classes. Since many parents are uncertain of the calendar age of their children, an Indian doctor issues certificates that establish the age of children for school purposes.

School statistics for 1979–1980 indicate that more than twice as many boys as girls attended school: 597 boys and 260 girls. Of these, 222 boys and 91 girls were from rural villages near Hamra; the remainder were from Hamra itself. Table 1 shows attendance at the girls' school. From its opening until 1979, enrollment was fairly steady. The sharp increase in 1979–1980 is directly attributable to the opening of a separate girls' school and the employment of more teachers.

Table 1
Girls' School Enrollment, Hamra

Academic Year	Students
1975 (½ year only)	175
1975–1976	175
1976–1977	not available
1977–1978	188
1978–1979	169
1979–1980	260

Source: Interview, headmistress, girls' school, Hamra, June 15, 1980.

One difficulty with the available school statistics for Hamra is that they provide neither the age of students in each grade nor the high degree of attrition among students from grade to grade. Many girls in their teens entered in the first years after the school opened, only to drop out after a year or two in order to get married. According to the school's headmistress and women in Hamra, early marriage for girls continues to be the principal cause of the high dropout rate among primary school girls as opposed to the rate among boys. Thus, in 1979–1980, forty-two girls in primary school dropped out, but only four boys did so.

The status of the families of children attending school is unavailable from official sources, but it appears that children from shaykhly and wealthy families are much more likely to complete primary, intermediate, and, increasingly, secondary schooling; other students are much more prone to drop out of school. Of the eight girls studying at the intermediate level in Hamra in 1979–1980, I knew five personally, and they were all from the shaykhly-descent cluster. The heavy dropout rate among girls accounts for the nearly constant enrollment between 1975 and 1979, rather than an overall increase in the number of students as earlier enrollees moved to the upper grades and new students entered the system.

Among the shaykhly families, marriage is not necessarily an impediment to attending school. Two of the five shaykhly girls attending the intermediate school were married. The fact that the school bus for the girls' school was owned and driven by a young man from the shaykhly-descent cluster—one of their relatives—facilitated their mobility. The girls' school is located in the complex of government buildings away from the main oasis and on the other side of the market, making it virtually inaccessible for female students on foot. Despite the growing universality of access to education, persons of shaykhly descent continue to be more likely than others to complete their schooling. Nonetheless—and this is a recent change—the children of persons of the lowest status, those of slave descent, sit side by side with those of shaykhly descent in government schools.

Since education for women was introduced so recently to Hamra, it is still too soon to see its consequences for women after they have left school. For those who attend school only a year or two, as has been true for many women, the impact is minimal. Nasra, one of my neighbors, went to school for two years. During that time she began learning how to read and write modern Arabic. Since her marriage and the birth of her children, she has used her reading skills only in public recitals of the Quran, a skill she acquired earlier from attendance at a Quranic school. She has no access to newspapers or magazines because they are not distributed in Hamra.

Education appears to have a greater effect on those few who manage to attend the full primary school cycle and the intermediate one. I learned from conversations with these women, all of shaykhly descent, that possession of a diploma is seen as prestigious, something associated with high social rank. Attending school also provided them relief from the boredom and frustration associated with the de facto waiting period between their status of child and that of full adult. The idea of using skills acquired in school for any practical purpose, such as government service or higher studies elsewhere in Oman, is still too remote a possibility for these young women to discuss.

Some individual reactions make clear this uncertainty about the results of acquiring an education.

Thariyya spends her mornings in school and her afternoons caring for her numerous younger brothers. Her attitude toward school is negative. She finds nearly all subjects equally boring. Only English is less so, because the American Peace Corps volunteer does not hit her; corporal discipline is a pedagogical technique commonly employed by many of the Egyptian teachers. Socially Thariyya is still treated as a nonadult and thus has few visiting obligations. When guests show up, she often does not offer them dates and ready-made coffee herself. Instead, she takes advantage of her immature status and calls upon another adult in the household. On other occasions, such as when her paternal grandmother and aunt came visiting from Muscat, she showed herself to be gracious and a smooth conversationalist.

Adolescent gossip said that she is to marry a maternal cousin. In her conversation with other girls and women, she seems somewhat withdrawn, although very conscious of her shaykhly status. Obviously bright, she feels restricted by her nonadult status, her childcare responsibilities, and her indeterminate status as an educated woman who is still unmarried. Although uninterested in school, she continues to attend for the prestige it brings and for the lack of anything better to do.

Shaykha, also of shaykhly descent, has been married for two years but is still childless. Her husband works in Muscat and returns once a week to Hamra.

Unlike Thariyya, Shaykha likes certain subjects. Mathematics in particular gives her intellectual stimulation. Her household responsibilities are minimal, and she spends a lot of her time studying in the afternoon and sewing both for herself and for her home economics class. She has no plans for continuing her studies past the intermediate level (no higher level was available for women in Hamra at the time). Nor does she expect to work in an office or in teaching. She enjoys studying and has the free time to do so.

Muza has also been married for two years. She lives with Asila, her husband's mother, in one of the few newly constructed cement houses in Hamra's "old town." Her husband returns once a week from his job in the capital area. During the last months of my stay in Hamra, it was clear that ill feelings and tension were building between Muza and Asila, a widow with an only son, who wanted Muza to bear a child. Muza is a bright student and interested in her studies. Attending school provides her relief from a tense domestic situation, and she can make long visits to her mother every day.

Young women in Hamra hardly ever think of continuing their education beyond what is available in Hamra itself, nor do they view education as a means of entering a career, such as teaching. The idea of residing far from the family cluster in order to complete studies in the capital is simply not conceived as possible now, although hostels exist for male students to live away from their families. A shaykh in Hamra once told my husband that women, including his daughters, would be allowed to study abroad if the government could guarantee an adequately "protected" environment. So far, he felt, such an environment does not exist. Yet he welcomed the idea of advanced education for women.

Once married, women are under heavy social and psychological pressure to become pregnant quickly. Muza once said to me, "I must have a child by the time I am eighteen, or else my husband will take a second wife. And men *must* do so if they do not have children." Muza accepts men's desire to have sons, and for this reason she is worried because she is not yet pregnant.[3] Having a child, however, does not necessarily prevent a woman from attending school, provided that her family cluster can assume some of her household and childcare responsibilities.

A final important consideration is that these young women constitute the first generation to attend government schools; therefore, there are no locally available models for what women can do with education. All the teachers at the girls' school are foreigners. Most of them openly look down on the lifestyle of people in the oasis and rarely initiate social contact with Omanis. Increased contact between the young women of the interior and women of the coastal cities, where there is a fairly large number of Omani women, often of Baluchi, Luwati, or East African origin, working as teachers and administrators may eventually provide such models. Interviews by Helga Graham (1978) among the first generation of Qatari women in professions such as teaching, social work, and medicine indicate that the main ingredients for academic success are support from family members to study abroad, money, a strong personality, and an awareness of specific job openings, usually in government. Once a few women succeed in obtaining advanced degrees and their possession become prestigeful, it will become easier for other women to follow.

Traditional Medicine

Traditional medicine is in many ways related to the importance of children and childbearing, one of the main topics of this chapter. What are the options open to women if they do not have children? How do women cope with sick children? Until what age does a mother have control over the type of treatment a child will have in case of illness? How do women evaluate the available alternatives?

As the preceding discussions of schooling and the achievement of full adult status by women indicate, the pressure on women to bear children is enormous and makes every other pursuit, including education, secondary. A few older women, often of low status, give massages of the abdomen and lower back to women who want to have children. If this does not work, the next recourse is a visit to a doctor, usually of Indian or Pakistani origin, who specializes in cases of infertility. There are such doctors at Nizwa, some forty minutes away from Hamra by automobile. I do not know for certain the treatment used by these doctors, most of whom are at a disadvantage because of their having only a very rudimentary command of Arabic, but in some cases the medicine they prescribe is said to work. Other women terminate their treatments after a few visits, citing the expense involved and the lack of results. For these women, the last recourse for infertility (and for other maladies) is medicinal branding (*wasm;* pl., *wusūm*) of the abdomen and lower back, a method that continues to be highly regarded by men and women in the oasis. Although Omani women recognize that men can be infertile (and most women reminded me of this once they found out that my child was adopted), I learned of no traditional treatment for male infertility.

> December 3. I went to the mourning at Shaykh Ibrahim's. Very few visitors were present. One woman whom I did not know asked me what to do when one catches a cold. I told her about the most common remedies—aspirin, lots of liquids, and rest. She said that these remedies were not very effective and added that Omanis have a much more effective way of dealing with disease—branding, or burning with fire. I had not heard of the practice until then, and my astonishment showed on my face. I made her repeat her words to make sure that I understood her correctly. Then I commented, "What an extraordinary ['*ajīb*] remedy!" The younger women were delighted by my reaction, if for no other reason than it offered a distraction from the long

days of mourning. Everyone in the room began explaining to me how the treatment worked. Some younger women showed me the scars on their bodies. One went to a side room and came back with a brand to show me what they look like.

Most Omanis believe that medicinal branding is unique to Oman, although it is a form of treatment practiced elsewhere on the Arabian peninsula and in the Middle East and North Africa: in Bahrain (Hansen, 1968: 127), Saudi Arabia (Katakura, 1977: 66), the Hadhramaut (Stark, 1936: 139–140), and the Sudan (Boddy, 1982: 694). It is prevalent on Oman's Batina coast, including Suhar, as well as in the interior. A technique that might be related to branding is medicinal tattooing, practiced in Iran by both pastoral nomads and villagers.[4] Women in Hamra told me that branding is employed for a whole range of serious diseases (amrāḍ thaqīla) in cases where the Western-type medical help is unavailable or is unsuccessful. Hospitals are believed by many women to be most suitable for the less serious diseases (amrāḍ khafīfa). Given the limited facilities of many hospitals and their uneven quality, this observation is not unrealistic.

For a wasm, a small branding iron is heated with matches until it is red-hot. Where the brand is applied on the body, and the size and shape of the brand used, depend upon the diagnosis, the gravity of the illness, and whether the patient is a child or an adult.

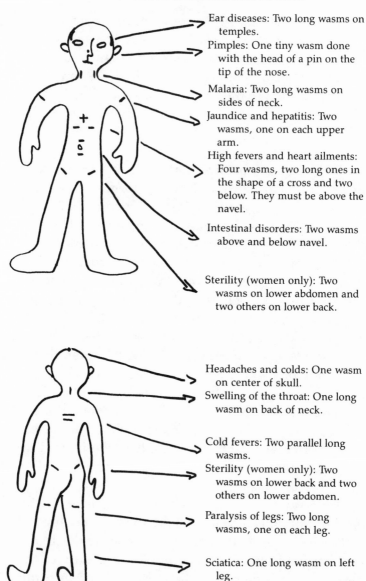

Ear diseases: Two long wasms on temples.

Pimples: One tiny wasm done with the head of a pin on the tip of the nose.

Malaria: Two long wasms on sides of neck.

Jaundice and hepatitis: Two wasms, one on each upper arm.

High fevers and heart ailments: Four wasms, two long ones in the shape of a cross and two below. They must be above the navel.

Intestinal disorders: Two wasms above and below navel.

Sterility (women only): Two wasms on lower abdomen and two others on lower back.

Headaches and colds: One wasm on center of skull.

Swelling of the throat: One long wasm on back of neck.

Cold fevers: Two parallel long wasms.

Sterility (women only): Two wasms on lower back and two others on lower abdomen.

Paralysis of legs: Two long wasms, one on each leg.

Sciatica: One long wasm on left leg.

Figure 12. Common medicinal brands in inner Oman.

Figure 12 illustrates the location, shape, and number of brands necessary for common diseases.

Serious diseases, such as sterility and heart problems, require more brands than other diseases. Once the skin is burned, olive oil is poured on the wound, which is left to heal by itself, usually leaving small-poxlike scars on the body. Women told me that if the branding is successful, there is an improvement in the patient's health as early as two or three days later. If a patient shows no improvement after the first treatment, a second one may then be given. The efficacy of treatment is rarely questioned. Younger educated shaykhly women such as Fatima acknowledged that branding can be dangerous, but she added that it seemed to work in many instances. If the treatment fails, it is because the brand is not applied in the right places or because the disease is more serious than was initially believed, requiring additional branding.

I knew two women in Hamra, both older women, who were considered experts in branding. One was from a prominent shaykhly household and also performed minor surgery. The other practitioner was from a low-status client tribal group, but she attracted patients regardless of their status because of her reputation for success. There were also men skilled in branding, although my husband learned of no man of shaykhly status who possessed such skills.

The incident involving minor surgery depicted in Chapter 4 indicates the social context in which traditional medicine is practiced. No strict privacy separates the sick person, the mother or guardian if the patient is a minor, and the medical practitioner from other persons. Traditional medicine is practiced within the family cluster. Family members are free to show an interest in what is going on and even to play an active role, as is the case for branding. The operation I witnessed took place in a side room but with some younger members of the family cluster watching. The door was left open, so that women in the next room were aware of what was going on in there. No one paid particular attention to the cries because their help was not needed. Only a few curious young women watched the operation.

There are similarities between the scene I witnessed and the descriptions of branding that I was given, although I was unable to see one during my stay in Hamra. Family members are often actively involved. Several young married shaykhly women told me how they were caught by surprise by their mothers, sisters, or other close family members and how they were forced into being branded. There was a hint of pride in their voices as they described how up to twenty women had to hold them down because they screamed so hard and tried to wrench free. I did not live within hearing distance of a house where branding occurred; so I cannot attest to these screams. My guess is that these accounts of loud screaming are exaggerated. Nonetheless, in a country where one usually speaks in a soft tone and where emotional displays are muted if they occur at all, be it in the marketplace or at coffee-drinking sessions, where one tries not to hinder the will of another, and where the body is completely covered and considered very private, these descriptions of the use of force on young adults, often already married, and of the uncovering of parts of the body in order to brand them are dramatic occurrences.

Whether a female is a child aged twenty months or a woman twenty years old, the mother maintains control over her body. By various tactics, including in some cases the use of force, she can oblige her daughter to be treated either for specific diseases of for more general ailments. "My daughter cried a lot," a woman answered when I asked why she had had her branded. The six-month-old infant had been suffering from intestinal disorders, and soon afterward the mother reported that her health improved. "My daughter is weak," another woman answered, talking of a twenty-year-old woman. Her daughter had given birth to four children in rapid succession, three of whom had died. She seemed anemic and frail, and she showed me parts of her body that were covered with the scars of past brandings.

Men, on the other hand, told my husband that they always gave their consent before undergoing treatment, at least once they were no longer infants, and denied ever being tricked or forced into it. A plausible explanation for the fact that some young shaykhly women made such a point of their resistance to being branded and of the large number of persons who had to restrain them is that it demonstrated the size of their family cluster and its willingness to come to their assistance. Not all women in Hamra have family clusters with twenty or so female members available to restrain them if they strenuously resist a branding. Most nonshaykhly women were reticent with me about their experiences with branding. They, too, claimed to be pressured into it by their mothers and other family members, but they did not emphasize this aspect or elaborate on the number of persons present.

Many women in Hamra are aware that there are better medical facilities in the capital area and outside of Oman. I returned to America with our daughter earlier than expected because Amal had developed an intestinal disorder, a problem she shared just then with many Omani children. Women of the oasis easily understood my decision to leave. Indeed, one shaykhly woman quietly asked me whether I would take with me her infant daughter who had the same problem. I looked at her, carefully containing her emotions behind a blank face and slightly rigid posture as she cradled her sickly daughter. "Yes, I would like to," I began. We then both remained silent, knowing that words were useless. Two years later, I learned from a student from Hamra who was studying in the U.S. that the child had been treated at the Nizwa hospital and was doing well. An older son, however, had died of scarlet fever.

NOTES

1. Compare Wright (1981: 138), who reports that in a village of central Iran, families having many brothers and sons have greater potential strength, although it is more difficult for them to maintain the mutual confidence upon which that strength rests.

2. Compare Siegel's (1969: 161–162) study of a Muslim community in Atjeh, Sumatra, where women are considered adults only after the birth of their first child.

3. I received a letter in 1983 from a shaykhly woman announcing that Muza and Shaykha had both given birth to daughters. The two women were also planning to continue their studies in the secondary school in Hamra.

4. Lois Beck, personal communication.

8.

HAMRA:
PAST AND PRESENT

I N a book intended only for an academic audience, an historical section normally comes first. In this study, it seems more natural to put it at the end. It was only after experiencing the society and community of Hamra for some time that I could interpret the significance of historical change.

Fifteen years ago Hamra formed a tightly knit community. The unity and cohesiveness have not disappeared, but the oasis is rapidly losing its social and spatial compactness. In the recent past, oasis inhabitants were linked by a common lifestyle, dependence on the falaj for water and their livelihood, a shared tribal identity, and intricate, overlapping ties of kinship, neighborliness, and patron-clientship. This cohesiveness was clearly visible in the physical layout of the oasis, with most of its households located close to one another in the hara, the main part of town.

Figure 13. Overview of Hamra. The small mosque adjacent to the head of the falaj is in the foreground. A cement house for one of the shaykhs is under construction behind it.

Until the mid-twentieth century, Hamra was a regional center of some importance. In 1826, the leading lineage of the 'Abriyin tribe, the Awlad Zahran, moved from 'Iraqi, an oasis near the town of 'Ibri, to settle in Hamra (Wilkinson, 1969: 157), thereby establishing Hamra as the tribal capital. Since the late eighteenth century, members of the Awlad Zahran lineage have constituted the tribe's political, economic, and religious elite. Half a dozen individuals from this lineage are today the largest landowners, possessing half the agricultural land in Hamra itself and large tracts of land elsewhere. Several shaykhly men earlier played leading roles in the administration of the twentieth-century Ibadi imamate (1913–1955), the center of which was located in Nizwa.[1] Until very recently, the majority of educated persons were of shaykhly descent.

The remaining population of the oasis belongs to other, less powerful lineages of the 'Abriyin and to client tribal groups. Client tribal groups are weaker tribes that at some time in the past sought protection from the 'Abriyin in exchange for payment in goods and labor. Another category of clients of shaykhly households are the day laborers (bidars) who take care of the falaj and date-palm trees. Many are said to be non-Arab descendants of peasant cultivators who traditionally tended the irrigated orchards in inner Oman and who gradually became incorporated into the present-day tribal system (Wilkinson, 1977: 142). Most oasis dwellers are highly uncertain about such matters. Some bidars say that they belong to the 'Abriyin tribe, although when they are in the presence of shaykhs, they are more likely to specify that they are actually from a client tribal group. Finally, there are the khuddam, slaves who were acquired by shaykhly men to serve as laborers and as reliable and trusted retainers. In the nineteenth century, some slaves were presented by the sultan to prominent shaykhs in order to gain their political support. Many slaves were freed after a lifetime of faithful service or on the death of their master (Cooper, 1977: 34–37). Even when formally set free, however, ex-slaves and their descendants continued to be regarded as khuddam and retained a low status in the community.

Not all slaves were of African origin. After 1902, when slavetrading with East Africa was virtually halted, some coastal towns on the Gulf imported slaves instead from Baluchistan (Landen, 1967: 152). A few were from other regions of Oman, including persons captured by marauding Bedouin groups who were subsequently sold into slavery (Wikan, 1982: 43; Barth, 1983: 175, 184–187). In spite of several treaties signed in the nineteenth century between Oman and the British government, traffic in slaves and domestic slavery continued in some parts of the Gulf area until the 1950s (Hawley, 1970: 136).

By the 1860s, the Gulf economic environment became seriously undermined by the introduction of Western-controlled goods and steam navigation. These innovations rapidly altered economic conditions in coastal Oman. In the interior, changing patterns of trade and political domination contributed to the decline and eventual disappearance of local economic activities, including the cultivation of cotton (Nizwa) and the production of cotton textiles, the making of brassware and copperware, and the manufacture of firearms. Cheap cotton from Bombay and the United States and superior firearms imported from the West totally displaced local manufacture of these products (Landen, 1967: 145–146; also Miles, 1910: 176).

Oman, including the interior, was further hurt economically by the declining demand for dates, one of its chief agricultural exports. Some causes of this decline were competition from other date-producing areas (including North Africa, Iraq, and California), currency fluctuations, and changes in eating habits (Wilkinson, 1977: 29–31). All the oases in Oman suffered from these economic currents.

Before the introduction of motor transport in the mid-1950s, Hamra was a caravan entrepôt. Dates and limes were gathered there for export to the coast and abroad either through the Suma'il Gap or through a much shorter footpath, too dangerous for animals along part of the way, which led from Hamra to Rustaq, on the other side of the mountains. Imported goods were redistributed through the Hamra market to its hinterland. With the introduction of motor transport, Hamra's role as an economic entrepôt began to shrink rapidly. The oasis was not astride any major motor route, and camel caravans and trade on foot vanished almost immediately. Except for villagers in Hamra's immediate hinterland, most tribesmen found goods in neighboring markets less expensive and of greater variety.[2]

To supplement a livelihood that often was little more than subsistence, and that in years of drought could be even less, for over a century men from Hamra have been compelled to migrate to obtain work. Until the 1950s, migrations were necessarily long-term, with the favored destinations being Bahrain and Kuwait, Zanzibar and the East African littoral. Zanzibar and coastal East Africa were under Omani rule, and later under a dynasty of Omani origin, since the eighteenth century, making the region a logical destination for persons from the Omani inte-

rior. Many emigrants secured capital from tribal
shaykhs before they left, so that even separated by
such great distances, patron-client and tribal ties remained firm.[3] In general, however, persons of
shaykhly lineage did not seek to migrate. This pattern
began to change by the late 1930s. In 1939, a religious
scholar and tribal leader of the 'Abriyin left the interior
to accept appointment as a *qāḍi* for Sultan Sa'id bin
Taymur in Muscat. In the summer months the shaykh
returned to Hamra, where he saw after his estates and
resolved local disputes (Eickelman, in press). For
many years few persons of shaykhly descent followed
his lead, but after 1980, many shaykhs sought government sinecures in Muscat and elsewhere, commuting
back to the oasis on weekends to see their families and
look after their lands and other enterprises in Hamra
itself.

Several events in the 1950s drastically affected
matters in inner Oman. The first was Sultan Sa'id bin
Taymur's dramatic royal progress to Nizwa and the
other principal towns of the interior in 1955. The sultan's visit, his first (and last) to the region, signaled
the collapse of the imamate and the beginning of the
sultan's direct administration of the region. This rein-
tegration of the interior with the coast was followed in
1957 by a rebellion in the interior, intended to restore
rule by the imamate. It was effectively quelled only
with the aid of British forces in 1959. Finally, there was
the rapid economic transformation of neighboring
Gulf states by the discovery and large-scale exporta-
tion of oil. The insecurity and economic stagnation of

Oman, especially in the interior, and the economic opportunities made possible by oil revenues in neighboring states led to extensive emigration. From the mid- to late 1950s, Saudi Arabia was the primary destination of Omani emigrants. Saudi Arabia supported the imamate movement, accommodated many political refugees, and provided economic and educational opportunities to many others. Bahrain, Kuwait, and Qatar were other favored destinations, followed in the 1960s by Dubai and Abu Dhabi. Women and children remained behind in Oman. An immediate result of the accelerated emigration of this period was a further decline in date agriculture caused by a shortage of manpower. Another result, not as visible at first, was the loosening of patron-client ties between shaykhly households and persons from client tribal groups or the descendants of slaves who were migrant laborers.[4]

The last fifteen years of the reign of Sultan Sa'id bin Taymur were a period of hardship and isolation for the majority of the Omani population. Foreign travel for Omanis to pursue an education was almost always forbidden. Even much of the emigration for "coolie" work elsewhere in the Gulf had to be clandestine. The only foreigners allowed to visit the Omani interior in the 1950s and 1960s were a handful of contract British officers and oil company employees. Once commercial quantities of oil were discovered in Oman in 1964 and exports got under way in 1967, the sultan chose to move very slowly and not to embark on a program of rapid development like those that were taking place in the neighboring Gulf states. In

1959, as a condition for lending military support to the sultan to quell the rebellion in the interior, the British insisted that he establish a Development Department, for which the British bore the entire financial responsibility. In large part because of the sultan's indifference or active opposition, the achievements through "development" a decade later were slim: a few hundred kilometers of graded tracks, a primary school for boys that lacked both a curriculum and textbooks, and two experimental farms run by foreigners (Townsend, 1977: 68). In Hamra itself, through 1970, there was little to show of "development." The tribal shaykh obtained permission from the sultan to import at his own expense a small, gasoline-driven motor for a flour mill and a Land Rover, the only one in the oasis. A brother of the shaykh, a governor of the neighboring oasis of Bahla, possessed a second vehicle. A few persons owned portable radio receivers.

The coming to power of Sultan Qabus bin Sa'id in July 1970 brought rapid changes to the interior. The way was open to intensive investment in infrastructure and development projects for the entire country. From a long-term perspective, the changes initiated in 1970 consolidated transformations under way since the 1950s. Hamra and other oases in the interior quickly became minor administrative satellites of the government in Muscat.[5] Since the construction of a network of paved roads linking Hamra to other cities of the interior and the coast and to neighboring Abu Dhabi, merchants in Hamra can no longer effectively compete with larger market centers elsewhere. Local

crafts are rapidly disappearing, and agricultural production is likewise decreasing owing to a shortage of
agricultural manpower. Falaj agriculture has suffered
in particular from the loss of manpower since few
young men are willing or even able to maintain the
complex irrigation system. Repairs are still made, but
everyone hopes that extensive repairs will not be required. Many small oases, including some in the region of Hamra, are dying out because of the villagers'
inability to repair their falaj or to cope with long periods of drought (compare Birks, 1977a, 1977b). The diet
of much of the population has also been altered. Former staples of the interior included dried shark meat
(Cox, 1925: 198) and fried locusts (Miles, 1910: 422). I
have seen some children eat locusts as snacks, but
now a variety of fresh and frozen foods are available,
brought from the coast by refrigerated trucks. Canned
food is also available.

As opportunities for work have become available
in Oman over the last decade, the number of men
leaving in search of work elsewhere has declined.
Nonetheless, most attractive opportunities for work
are away from the interior. In 1980, 43 percent of
Hamra's male adults were employed away from the
oasis: in the army, in the capital, or in neighboring
Abu Dhabi (Eickelman, 1980a: 7). Improved communications enable most of these migrants to return to
Hamra weekly or monthly. Many young men, descendants of slaves in particular, were quick to join the
police and the army in the early 1970s, although
recruitment now appears to be roughly equal from

all sectors of the Omani population. Many others have taken advantage of educational opportunities in Oman, and a few have gone to Abu Dhabi. Some persons, mostly those of shaykhly descent, but others as well, have obtained work as administrators and clerks in the burgeoning governmental apparatus. The majority, however, have accepted semiskilled and unskilled work as drivers and guards.

In 1972 a direct presence of the central government was established in Hamra with the appointment of a governor. The fact that the governor's house was on the lands of the tribal shaykh and was connected to his electricity generator suggested that the governor had an uphill struggle to establish his authority. Relations between the tribal shaykh and the governor were cordial, but the tribal shaykh maintained a decisive local influence. In 1980–1981 the governor was a young man in his twenties from a shaykhly family of another oasis in the interior. He consulted with the tribal shaykh on every major decision, deferred to the local shaykh's knowledge of the nuances of local affairs, and spent much of his time lobbying for a transfer to Muscat.

In Hamra itself, the governor is the only "modern" employer. A total of ninety-four Omanis worked for the government in Hamra in 1980, and the majority of these employees were from Hamra itself (Eickelman, 1980a: 9). The ministries of the Interior, Land Affairs and Municipalities, Health, Justice, and Pious Endowments, Agriculture, and Education all had local offices. By 1982 a small post office was established. In some cases the government has supplemented rather than replaced locally provided institutions, such as pious endowments, Quranic schools, and traditional medicine, which coexists with modern health care. In other cases the government has provided services not previously available, including garbage removal, malaria prevention, and some agricultural assistance.

The establishment of modern governmental services has altered how the people of Hamra view their previously existing institutions. The Quranic school, for example, has become in essence a preschool, which children attend briefly before entering government school. If an illness is not cured or alleviated by modern medical care, then older forms of medicine are employed. Likewise, some people still prefer to start first with traditional curing and to use modern facilities (not always staffed locally with personnel of the highest caliber) as a last resort. In the past, a prolonged drought would have entailed extreme hardship. In the summer of 1980, when such a drought led to a dangerous fall in the level of the falaj, the government set up tanks for drinking water at strategic points along the falaj, filling them with water carried by tanker trucks from nearby wells.

A large foreign community now lives in Oman. In 1980, 16 percent of the population was foreign, but this proportion is still low when compared with neighboring countries in the Gulf region. The foreign community falls into three main categories. Most skilled advisers and senior management come from Europe. Middle-ranking officials and teachers are mostly from

India, Jordan, and Egypt, with the Egyptians pre-
dominating in government employment. Commercial
enterprises generally prefer middle-level employees
from the Indian subcontinent. Unskilled and semiskilled construction workers, servants, and general
laborers are almost all recruited from India, Pakistan,
Bangladesh, and Sri Lanka (Birks and Sinclair, 1977a:
43). Although many Omanis are capable of filling
these posts, they prefer to work in neighboring Gulf
states, where salaries are significantly higher, leaving
foreigners to fill the equivalent posts in Oman. The
distribution of these foreigners throughout Oman is
uneven. In the capital area, population estimates indicate, there is nearly one foreigner for every Omani
national. In Nizwa, in contrast, the foreign population, mostly unskilled workers and shopkeepers, is
estimated at no more than one in thirteen (Directorate-General of Statistics, 1980).[6]

In Hamra, there were 150 foreigners in 1980 (Eickelman, 1980a: 9). Two-thirds of this number were
Egyptian and Jordanian schoolteachers and their families. They lived in special housing outside the oasis
proper and returned each summer to their countries
of origin. The remaining foreigners, who also lived
outside the oasis proper, were contract workers from
India and Pakistan who were electricians, carpenters,
mechanics, and barbers or were engaged in construction work. One served as driver for the tribal shaykh.
In recent years two shaykhs have pioneered in using
Indian and Pakistani labor to tend cash crops in fields
irrigated by well water outside the oasis. This trend

toward using foreign labor in fields not fed by falaj water is becoming prevalent throughout Oman. There is still strong resistance to employing foreigners in areas served by falaj irrigation. The people of Hamra say this is due to foreigners' lack of the knowledge necessary to work in falaj-irrigated fields and with date-palm trees. Further compelling reasons may be that such fields are adjacent to Omani housing, are worked sometimes by Omani women, and are criss-crossed with paths used intensively by women. Allowing foreign men into this part of the oasis is an innovation that the people of the oasis are unwilling to accept.

There have been significant shifts in Hamra's spatial layout since the early 1970s. Half a mile from the oasis proper, the road leading away to Nizwa and Bahla intersects with one going to the mountain village of Misfa. Most of the government offices are clustered around this crossroad. These include the offices of the governor, the qadi (who since 1980 was himself of the Awlad Zahran shaykhly lineage), housing for these two officials, and primary and intermediate schools for boys and girls. A few shops are nearby, and by 1983 a bank and a post office had been added to this cluster.

By the late 1970s, many shopkeepers had begun to abandon the old market, itself located at the edge of the falaj-irrigated oasis and mud-brick "old town." The old location was inaccessible to motor traffic. Shops now are located along the main road between the old market and the cluster of government buildings not far away, but in cement-brick buildings with metal shutters. The old market is still the center for the auction of animals, local agricultural produce, water rights, and bulk sales of fruits and vegetables trucked in from elsewhere. The new shops have fixed prices, although some clients can be favored over others and it is common to grant extensive credit to retain loyal customers. These shops carry a range of canned and cold-store goods, packaged rice from Pakistan, plastic and hardware goods, building materials, ready-made clothes, and bicycles and sewing machines from the People's Republic of China. There is even a shop, capitalized by an Omani entrepreneur but managed by the husband of an Egyptian schoolteacher, that carries the food preferred by Egyptians. There are Indian barbers and tailors, working on contract to local Omanis, and the old, shaykh-owned flour mill, now run by an Indian contract worker.

By laws established soon after the "new era" inaugurated by Sultan Qabus bin Sa'id, every Omani citizen is entitled, upon token payment, to plots of land for housing, agriculture, and commerce. The immediate consequence for Hamra is that much of the land along the main road and along its main tributaries has been staked out into plots. Competition was intense for acquiring commercial plots around the new government quarters, which local entrepreneurs rightly sensed would quickly appreciate in value. As for the land staked out for residential use, some of the best plots and the most imposing houses have gone to persons of shaykhly descent, some of whom occupy high posts in the judiciary and the palace bureaucracy. Other houses are much more modest, their owners seeking to rent them to the government for use by foreign schoolteachers so that they can use the revenues to pursue other projects. Most houses are in various stages of completion. Each time the owner has the capital to add part of a wall, iron doors or shutters, or other conveniences, another addition is made to the house.

Nonshaykhly households are the most avid to take advantage of new housing away from the mud-brick old town. The extent of relocation can be seen indirectly from the 1980 census of Hamra (Eickelman, 1980a: 15). At that time, 60 percent of the households surveyed in Hamra had not moved in the lifetime of the head of the household, 12 percent had moved to nearby locations in the hara, and 28 percent had moved to the periphery of the oasis, where the plots for new housing are located. Since cement-block construction was prohibited before 1970, well water was much scarcer before then, and there were very few mud-brick houses in peripheral locations. Almost all the moves to peripheral locations have occurred since 1970. Many of the families who chose to move left their housing in the center of the hara, an area with poor access to water. By 1980, much of this section was in a state of disrepair, with many houses abandoned or in danger of collapsing.

Shaykhly households, in direct contrast with non-shaykhly ones, invest in repairing their old, imposing mud-brick houses and construct adjacent or nearby cement additions. Their old location is an excellent one. It is located next to the head of the falaj, the traditional source of all drinking water. Falaj water is cleanest near the head, making it much more convenient for washing clothes and dishes. Moreover, the tall palm trees of the oasis gardens cool some of the nearby housing, and the shaykhly households all have small houses in the orchards, which they can choose to use in the heat of the afternoon. The modern cement houses at the new peripheral locations have no such amenities and afford little protection against the heat. Inhabitants of the shaykhly households continue to live within walking distance of one another. They are able to engage in the frequent visiting necessary for maintaining strong family ties.

The recent shifts in Hamra's spatial layout are directly related to wider currents of economic and social change. Economically, the role of migratory labor is much more important than it was even a decade ago. Likewise, goods and services previously unavailable or sporadically obtainable only by the elite of the oasis are now taken for granted by the entire population. The falaj still plays an important role in oasis life, but access to its irrigation water is no longer an overriding concern for many households. Tribal warfare ceased many decades ago, and with it the necessity vanished for housing to be protectively clustered. New divisions are also beginning to emerge among the population. As Wilkinson (1980: 129) notes, there is an emerging distinction between those who benefit from the income derived from wage labor elsewhere and those

who do not. Persons with steady wage labor elsewhere can afford new housing, motor transport, generators, and refrigerators. The standard of living of
other households remains much as it was ten years
ago. This new economic differentiation crosscuts the
old categories based on descent and freeman/slave
status. Moreover, patron-client ties with shaykhly
households are beginning to erode. Once the maintenance of such ties was a necessity. This is no longer
the case.

Nonetheless, inhabitants of Hamra maintain with
pride their common identity as 'Abriyin. One way that
descendants of slaves assert higher status (upon pro-
motion in the ranks of the police or army, for example)
is to place banners outside their houses on feast days
proclaiming their best wishes for the inhabitants of
the oasis, and they sign their names in such a way as
to indicate that they are members of the 'Abriyin tribe,
not just its ex-slaves. Such an assertion of new status
would have been unheard of a decade ago. Now it occasions comment from some oasis dwellers, but never in
public. Others have sought to challenge the leadership of the Awlad Zahran lineage, but not to challenge
the notion of tribal identity itself.

There has been only minimal permanent emigration from Hamra since 1970. The high cost of housing
in the capital area, the continued value placed on the
strength of family ties, and the explicit desire to live
close to "known" and trusted persons have induced
most households to remain in Hamra. Only a few men
have moved their households to the capital area, and

even these commute back to Hamra regularly. Rarely are they gone for over a month. For households that now live primarily in the capital, part of their prestige and status derives from maintaining a residence and agricultural lands in Hamra.[7] One of the reasons why the costs of falaj-irrigated land, water, and date palms have skyrocketed in recent years is that they have become important as symbols of social status.

Women's visiting networks continue to be an important source of oasis unity. Even when excellent housing is available elsewhere, as is the case for workers in Abu Dhabi, most men prefer to leave their wives and children in Hamra, and most wives agree with this decision. Once I asked a woman whether she wanted to take her children and go to live with her husband in Abu Dhabi. Her answer was vehemently negative: "I do not want to live alone. I have no family there, no people to visit." Her tone and the quickness of her response suggested that she had already considered the possibility of moving and had rejected it. For most oasis dwellers, women's visiting networks are too valued to be abandoned.

The continued presence and influence in Hamra of the shaykhly family cluster contribute to the ongoing unity of the oasis. Part of the income of most shaykhly households now derives from the work of some family members in the capital area. Some shaykhs have invested in lands and housing in the capital area. But there they compete for work and prestige with many other persons, not all of whom are of tribal origin. In Hamra they remain at the top of

local society. They continue to be the largest landowners, and they predominate in such local activities
as the marketing of cash crops, the construction of
government buildings, and the contracting of government services, such as the minibuses to deliver children and teachers to school. They also furnish capital
to many local shopkeepers and manage other local
enterprises. The shaykhly lineage continues to be of
pivotal importance in Hamra, both to the clients of
shaykhs and their households and to those households antagonistic to them.

Hamra is clearly not a dying oasis, but its local
economy continues to stagnate and to depend more
and more on wage labor elsewhere. Given the high
birthrate in Oman and the lack of local economic opportunities, permanent and semipermanent emigration is bound to increase in coming years. The people
most likely to leave first are those with no land or
economic future in the oasis, those with the least to
lose. The children of shaykhly households have been
the first to realize the advantage of completing their
education instead of leaving school earlier to obtain
ready employment as drivers or low-level clerks.
Those who complete higher education necessarily see
their careers away from the oasis and have become
oriented more toward national concerns than local
ones. As higher education is increasingly valued by all
levels of society, the trend toward moving away from
the oasis by choice or to seek a career will no doubt
accelerate.

The people of Hamra have held on to their way of
life and view it as the "right" one. They continue to

value the primacy of strong family ties and residence in the midst of relatives and trusted neighbors. Their notions of Islam, sociability, and propriety remain meaningful interpretations of, and guides for, the social world. Despite the rapidly changing economic context in which they live, they do not feel that their basic values are being threatened or eroded. Their social and economic environment is rapidly changing, but the values by which they make sense of their lives are self-renewing and remain as vital today as they were in the past.

NOTES

1. For an analysis of the tribal system of inner Oman and its relationship to the Ibadi imamate, see Wilkinson (1969; cf. Eickelman, 1980b). For a discussion of the changing relations among tribal shaykhs, the imamate government, and the sultanate, see Eickelman (in press).

2. Speece (1982) provides an analysis of economic life in Oman in the nineteenth and early twentieth centuries.

3. Compare Bujra's (1971: 75) comment that emigrant labor from South Arabia before World War II to Malaysia and southeast Asia was provided mostly by the weathier members of the *sāda* class, descendants of the Prophet, who could afford the traveling expenses.

4. Compare Lindholm (1982: 102–103), who states that despite the increasing importance of emigrant labor and remittances among the Swat Pukhtun, some emigrant workers continue to work at least part-time for the *khans*, their patrons. It is the patrons themselves who complain about the burden of client ties and seek ways to break away from them. With the growing importance of a cash economy and the increased costs of labor, the cost of providing food, shelter, gifts, and protection to clients has become too much of a burden for them.

5. See Wilkinson's (1980) and Eickelman's (1983) analyses of changes in the structure of village life in Oman. Eickelman (1983) discusses a village in the immediate vicinity of Hamra.

6. Especially for the interior regions, these estimates are tentative and must be treated with caution.

7. The value placed upon housing and land in one's oasis of origin is also prevalent in Saudi Arabia. In discussing my work in 1983, a Saudi student commented that Jidda, his own town, becomes empty of Saudis on major Muslim holidays as people return to their villages of origin, where they maintain houses and property.

GLOSSARY

Terms are defined according to principal local usage in Oman.

'abāya	A long, black cloak that covers the entire body; worn by women of some groups in Oman.
'azā'	Period of consolation, or mourning.
bayt al-'urubā	Literally, "house of foreigners." Term used primarily by women to denote a guest room. See *sābla*.
bidār; pl., bayādīr	Agricultural day laborer.
dishdāsha	Long, neck-to-ankle tunic.
falaj; pl., aflāj	Irrigation system of gently sloping tunnels and narrow conduits that conduct water to lands suitable for cultivation.
ḥāra	Literally, "quarter." In Hamra, denotes the main cluster of mud-brick houses.
ḥayyān	Family cluster. Used as both singular and plural.
'Id al-Fiṭr	Religious holiday marking the end of Ramadan.

'Id al-Kabīr, al-	Literally, "the Great Feast"; commemorates the sacrifice of Abraham.
imām	Spiritual and temporal leader of the Ibadi community (until 1955); prayer leader.
jamā'a	Community; group.
khādim; pl. khuddām	Person descended from slave ancestors.
khajal	Constraint caused by concern over doing something improper; shyness.
khatma	Public recital of the Quran.
laysu	Multicolored shawl worn by women.
mahr	Bridewealth.
mālka	Reading of a marriage contract.
mawla; pl., mawāli	Person or tribal group with client status.
mjāza	Washing house for women.
maṣalla	Place of prayer.
murabbiya	Twenty-five-day visiting period after the birth of a child.
qāḍi	Religious judge.
qiyāḍ	Literally, "exchange." Also denotes an agreement whereby two households each exchange a son and a daughter in marriage to minimize payment of bridewealth.
Ramaḍān	Lunar month of fasting.
sabla	Guest room. See also *bayt al-'urubā.*
wāli	Governor.
wasm; pl., wusūm	Medicinal brand.
wizār	Long cotton or polyester cloth wrapped by men around their waists. Worn without dishdasha

for informal occasions or under
dishdasha for more formal ones.

zifāf   Wedding ceremony.

BIBLIOGRAPHY

Altorki, Soraya. "Family Organization and Women's Power in Urban Saudi Arabian Society." *Journal of Anthropological Research* 33: 277–287 (1977).

———. "Milk-kinship in Arab Society: An Unexplored Problem in the Ethnography of Marriage." *Ethnology* 19: 233–244 (1980).

Ammar, Hamad. *Growing Up in an Egyptian Village.* London: Routledge & Kegan Paul, 1954.

Anderson, Jon. "Social Structure and the Veil: Comportment and the Composition of Interaction in Afghanistan." *Anthropos* 77: 397–420 (1982).

Ardener, Shirley. "Ground Rules and Social Maps for Women: An Introduction." In *Women and Space: Ground Rules and Social Maps,* edited by Shirley Ardener, pp. 11–34. London: Croom Helm, 1981.

Barth, Fredrik. *Sohar: Culture and Society in an Omani Town.* Baltimore and London: The Johns Hopkins University Press, 1983.

Birks, J. S. "Diqal and Muqayda: Dying Oases in Arabia." *Journal of Economic and Social Geography* 68: 145–151 (1977a).

———. "The Reaction of Rural Populations to Drought: A Case Study from South East Arabia." *Erdkunde* 31: 299–305 (1977b).

———, and C. A. Sinclair. "Country Case Study: The Sultanate of Oman." Durham: University of Durham, Department of Economics, International Migration Project, 1977, mimeo.

———, and C. A. Sinclair. "Aspects of the Demography of the Sultanate of Oman." Durham: University of Durham, Department of Economics, International Migration Project, 1977, mimeo.

Boddy, Janice. "Womb as Oasis: The Symbolic Context of Pharaonic Circumcision in Rural Northern Sudan." *American Ethnologist* 9: 682–698 (1982).

Bonine, Michael E. "Aridity and Structure: Adaptations of Indigenous Housing in Central Iran." In *Desert Housing: Balancing Experience and Technology for Dwelling in Hot Arid Zones*, edited by Kenneth N. Clark and Patricia Paylore, pp. 193–218. Tucson: University of Arizona, Office of Arid Lands, 1980.

Bujra, Abdalla S. *The Politics of Stratification: A Study of Political Change in a South Arabian Town.* Oxford: Clarendon Press, 1971.

Cooper, Frederick. *Plantation Slavery on the East Coast of Africa.* New Haven, Conn., and London: Yale University Press, 1977.

Cox, Sir Percy. "Some Excursions in Oman." *The Geographical Journal* 66: 193–227 (1925).

Eickelman, Dale F. "Time in a Complex Society: A Moroccan Example." *Ethnology* 16: 39–55 (1977).

———. "Hamra Social Survey, 1980." Unpublished report submitted to the Ministry of Social Affairs and Labour, Muscat (1980a).

____. "Religious Tradition, Economic Domination and Political Legitimacy: Morocco and Oman." *Revue de l'Occident Musulman et de la Méditerranée* 19: 17–30 (1980b).

____. "Omani Village: The Meaning of Oil." In *The Politics of Middle Eastern Oil*, edited by John Peterson. Washington, D.C.: The Middle East Institute, 1983, pp. 211–219.

____. "From Theocracy to Monarchy: Authority and Legitimacy in Inner Oman, 1935–1957." *The International Journal of Middle East Studies* 17 (1985) (in press).

Geertz, Hildred. "The Vocabulary of Emotion: A Study of Javanese Socialization Processes." *Psychiatry* 22: 225–237 (1959).

Gilsenan, Michael. *Recognizing Islam: Religion and Society in the Modern Arab World*. New York: Pantheon, 1982.

Graham, Helga. *Arabian Time Machine: Self-portrait of an Oil State*. London: Heinemann, 1978.

Hansen, Henny Harald. *Investigations in a Shi'a Village in Bahrain*. Copenhagen: The National Museum of Denmark, 1968.

Hawley, Donald. *The Trucial States*. London: George Allen and Unwin, Ltd., 1970.

Joseph, Suad. "Working Class Women's Networks in a Sectarian State: A Political Paradox." *American Ethnologist* 10: 1–22 (1983).

Kanafani, Aida Sami. *Aesthetics and Ritual in the United*

Arab Emirates. The Anthropology of Food and Personal Adornment Among Arabian Women. Beirut: American University of Beirut, 1983.

Katakura, Motoko. *Bedouin Village: A Study of a Saudi Arabian People in Transition.* Tokyo: University of Tokyo Press, 1977.

Landen, Robert G. *Oman since 1856: Disruptive Modernization in a Traditional Arab Society.* Princeton: Princeton University Press, 1967.

Lindholm, Charles. *Generosity and Jealousy: The Swat Pathans of Northern Pakistan.* New York: Columbia University Press, 1982.

Melville, Herman. *Typee. A Peep at Polynesian Life.* New York: The Library of America, 1983 [orig. 1846].

Miles, S. B. "On the Border of the Great Desert: A Journey in Oman." *The Geographical Journal* 36: 159–178, 405–425 (1910).

Nelson, Cynthia. "Public and Private Politics: Women in the Middle Eastern World." *American Ethnologist* 1: 551–563 (1974).

Sciama, Lidia. "The Problem of Privacy in Mediterranean Anthropology." In *Women and Space: Ground Rules and Social Maps,* edited by Shirley Ardener, pp. 89–111. London: Croom Helm, 1981.

Siegel, James. *The Rope of God.* Berkeley and Los Angeles: University of California Press, 1969.

Simmel, Georg. *The Sociology of Georg Simmel,* translated and edited by Kurt H. Wolff. New York: The Free Press, 1964.

Speece, Mark. "Sultan and Imam: An Analysis of Economic Dualism in Oman." Unpublished M.A.

thesis, University of Arizona, Department of Oriental Studies, 1982.

Stark, Freya. *The Southern Gates of Arabia: A Journey in the Hadhramaut.* London: John Murray, 1936.

_____. *A Winter in Arabia.* New York: E. P. Dutton and Co., 1940.

Sultanate of Oman, Directorate-General of Statistics. 1980. Unpublished census estimates.

Townsend, John. *Oman: The Making of a Modern State.* New York: St Martin's Press, 1977.

UNICEF, Gulf Area Office. "Beliefs and Practices Related to Health, Nutrition and Child Rearing in Two Communities of Oman. Part I. A Demographic Overview of Households in Nizwa and Sohar." Abu Dhabi: UNICEF Gulf Area Office, 1973, mimeo.

Wikan, Unni. *Behind the Veil in Arabia: Women in Oman.* Baltimore and London: The Johns Hopkins University Press, 1982.

Wilkinson, John C. "Arab Settlement in Oman: The Origins and Development of the Tribal Pattern and Its Relationship to the Imamate." Unpublished Ph.D. dissertation, University of Oxford, 1969.

_____. *Water and Tribal Settlement in South-East Arabia: A Study of the Aflāj of Oman.* Oxford: Clarendon Press, 1977.

_____. "Changes in the Structure of Village Life in Oman." In *Social and Economic Development in the Arab Gulf,* edited by Tim Niblock, pp. 122–134. London: Croom Helm, 1980.

Wright, Susan. "Place and Face: Of Women in Dosh-
man Ziari, Iran." In *Women and Space: Ground
Rules and Social Maps,* edited by Shirley Ardener,
pp. 136–157. London: Croom Helm, 1981.

INDEX